The Character of the Church

FIRST PRINTING

Billy Crone

Cover Design:
CHRIS TAYLOR

To my sister, Terri.

*Not only did God plan for you to be my earthly sister
but He also decreed that one day
you'd also be my heavenly sister.*

*As a true sister in the Lord, God worked it out
that you would be in California just in time
to disciple me as a brand new Christian
only a few days old.*

*It was you, Terri, that God used
to help me take my first steps as a baby Christian,
and lead me by the hand
to become a part of this thing
called Church life.*

*For these things and many more, I praise the
awesome sovereignty and profound wisdom
of God Almighty for you.
I love you.*

Contents

Preface

After I had become a Christian for a few years, I noticed a strange phenomenon in the Church of Jesus Christ. Many of my fellow brothers and sisters in Christ were flocking to the Church of Saint Mattress with Pastor I.B. Snoozin' of the Bedside Sheets Assembly. They would have a run in with other Christians, or those claiming to be Christians, and/or Church leadership and get fed up with what they saw; so they simply checked out, refused to get involved any longer, and became what I call "Lone Ranger" Christians. They turned their backs on the Church and decided to try to live the Christian life on their own, even though our Lord Jesus Christ has designed His Church to function "together" with other believers. They went in search of the pipe dream called "the perfect Church."

But what I tell people is that if you ever find the perfect Church, you and I better not go there because we'll mess it up! The point being this: read the New Testament. What were the letters written to the Churches for? They were written to address problems in the Churches! Therefore, the Church of Jesus Christ has always had problems and will continue to always have problems this side of heaven because we all still struggle with our imperfect old natures. With that in mind, may this book not only be a source of encouragement to you, but may it challenge you to get back on the front lines and serve God with the gifts He has given you. We need you!

However, this book is also for those of you out there who are living as horrible examples of Christians. First of all, the Bible declares that there are those who think they are saved but really are not. Think about that for a moment. Secondly, your ungodly behavior brings shame to the Holy Name of God. It is precisely this kind of living that not only keeps you from experiencing victory in your walk with Christ; it fuels people's hatred for Christianity. With that in mind, may this book not only be a source of encouragement to you, but may it challenge you to stop playing Church and start being the Church.

As always, when you are through reading this book, will you please READ YOUR BIBLE? I mean that in the nicest possible way. Enjoy and I'm looking forward to seeing you someday!

Billy Crone
Las Vegas, Nevada
2020

Chapter One

The Body of Christ

"The accident occurred on September 13, 1848 at a construction site on the East Coast of the United States. Phineas Gage was a foreman who on this day was making a bad decision.

You see, he was tamping dynamite into a hole with a huge three and a half foot iron rod that weighed over thirteen pounds. That's right. You guessed it. The jarring of the rod ignited the explosives and they blew the rod right out of the hole and through his head.

Phineas was taken to a doctor who immediately plugged the holes in his head and kept him under observation. Amazingly, Phineas Gage was not only still alive, but he was fully conscious. In fact, he experienced no apparent lasting physical handicaps.

However, mentally he had totally changed. Phineas Gage was once considered a mild-mannered gentlemen and a very capable foreman. But now he was transformed into an erratic, irritable, and profane man who continually cussed up a storm.

Because he was no longer a model employee, he used his status to get a job being displayed as a freak of nature at Barnum's Museum in New York City. It was only twelve years after his accident that Phineas Gage died in San Francisco."[1]

Now folks, I know this might be a tough question, but how many of you guys would like to have a steel bar go through your head? You know, something to do on a Saturday afternoon? People, the reason why I bring up the story of Phineas Gage is because it's one of the most famous examples of what's called TBI or in other words, Traumatic Brain Injury. As you heard with the case of Phineas, when a person has suffered a TBI they can either become a totally different person or frequently, they get amnesia and totally forget who they are. My point is this: What if I were to tell you that not thousands but millions of people right now are suffering from TBI and get this, they don't even know it! And here's the kicker. Can you guess who these people are? Hey, that's right! It's the American Church! How do I know? Because we've totally forgotten who we are!

People, the facts are half the time we not only acting like Practical Atheists, we're acting like we have practical amnesia! We don't even know who we are anymore! The problem is this. Having practical amnesia is not only detrimental to our walk with Christ, it keeps others from believing in Christ. Therefore, to avoid this atrocity of Christians living with practical amnesia by not knowing who they are; we're going to begin a new study from the Word of God on the people of God entitled, "**The Character of the Church.**"

People, it's pretty simple the **first thing** we need to know about the Church if we're going to stop living like we have practical amnesia is that **The Church is the Body of Christ**.

Colossians 1:15-18 "He is the image of the invisible God, the firstborn over all creation. For by Him all things were created: things in heaven and on earth, visible and invisible, whether thrones or powers or rulers or authorities; all things were created by Him and for Him. He is before all things, and in Him all things hold together. And He is the head of the body, the church; He is the beginning and the firstborn from among the dead, so that in everything He might have the supremacy."

Now folks, according to the text, it's pretty simple. Jesus is the Head and Chief Authority over the what? Not only the universe, but what? The Church, right? Why? Because we're the Body of Christ, right? Here's my point. Surely, we all know that, right? I mean, surely every Christian who has ever lived knows that we're the Body of Christ, right? Well, you'd think so, but apparently, we have some problems.

The **first problem** we have is we don't say the Church is the Body of Christ. No! We say **The Church is a Building**.

Matthew 16:18 "And I tell you that you are Peter, and on this rock I will build my church, and the gates of Hades will not overcome it."

Now folks, there you have it. According to our text we see the very first recorded Christian building program, right? I mean what did Jesus say there? He's going to build Himself a what? A Church, right? Therefore, He's got to be speaking about a big ol' building with a steeple and stained glass windows, right? Apparently it's going to be OSHA approved because not even Hell can knock this baby down, you know what I'm saying? That's right, for those of you who haven't caught on yet; yes, I'm being very sarcastic. Why? Because people, if you listen to most Christians talk, that's exactly what they're saying! They think the Church is a building instead of the Body of Christ!

Why in the world would Christians think we're a building instead of the Body of Christ? Hey, great question. I'm glad you asked. It's pretty simple. The **1ˢᵗ reason** is because **We Repeat What Others Say and Do**.

Oh, talk about your ultimate bad habit! People, we say all kinds of things that we have no idea where they came from, let alone if they're even true. For instance, how many times have you heard it said, "An apple a day keeps the doctor away?" Yeah, we say that all the time, don't we? But folks have you ever stopped to ask yourself where it came from or if it's even true? No, of course not! We repeat all kinds of things we know nothing about. People, the facts are the average apple has only .0004 ounces of vitamin C. The main ingredient of an apple seems to be sugar. Therefore we need to update the phrase to say, "An apple a day keeps the dentist coming our way!" So, why do we say it? Well, apparently back in the 1800's, apple sales began to drop and the apple growers blamed it on the Christians who kept saying the apple was responsible for the fall of man. So the farmers came up with the slogan to boost their sales and apparently it worked because we not only keep saying it, but we keep buying those apples to keep that doctor away![2]

Oh, but that's not all. How about this saying: Why do we say "God bless you" when somebody sneezes?" Have you ever stopped to think about that? Why do we say it only when somebody sneezes and not when they cough? In fact, one time in Bible College I tried it. I couldn't take it anymore. Every time somebody sneezed in class, fifteen super spiritual Christians would say, "God Bless you." I couldn't take it so I decided to test it out on a cough. You know, inquiring minds want to know. I waited for somebody to cough and declared out loud, "God Bless you!" Man, you wouldn't believe the looks I got. It was like I turned into the antichrist or something. It was as if people were saying, "What? Are you nuts or something? Don't you know that you are only supposed to say that when somebody sneezes?"

People my point is this. Why do we say this and where did it come from? Well, hey, thanks for asking. Apparently it started way back in the Dark Ages when people were very superstitious. Back then they thought a sneeze was caused either by demons leaving the body or it left one vulnerable for demons to enter the body. People would do two things. One, they would make the sign of the cross in front of the mouth, which is where we get the custom of covering our mouth when sneezing and the second thing they would do is say "God Bless you" as a way of asking God to protect them from demonic harm.[3]

People I think the point is pretty obvious here. We obviously repeat what others say all the time without even thinking about it, right?

Exactly! But that's not all. That's only half of it. We not only repeat what others say; but we do what others do without thinking about it, like this lady did:

"There was a husband and wife who had been married for a little while and the husband noticed that every time his wife would make meatloaf, she cut a portion of the meatloaf off on each side before she put it into the pan. For the life of him, he couldn't figure it out. To him, she was wasting perfectly good meat. So, he asked her why she lopped off both ends of the meatloaf before she stuck it into the pan.

To which she said, 'I don't know. That was the way my Mom always did it.'

So, they called up the mom and asked her why she lopped off both ends of the meatloaf before she put it into the pan. And she said, 'I don't know. That's the way your grandmother always did it.'

So finally, they tracked down the grandma and asked her why she lopped off both ends of the meatloaf before she stuck it into the pan. The grandma replied that back in her earlier days, the pan she had to cook meatloaf in was too small. So in order to get it to fit, she had to cut both ends off!"[4]

People, my point is this. I bet you we do all kinds of things just like that without thinking about it. For instance, maybe it's the way you decorate the Christmas tree every year, or maybe it's the way you set the table for supper, or maybe it's the way you discipline your kids. Whatever it is, it's obvious we do what others do all the time without even thinking about it, right? Exactly!

Here's my point. If we're not careful, this tendency to repeat what others say and do will spill over into what we say and do as Christians. If you don't believe me, let's take a test. If somebody asked you what you do on Sunday mornings what would you say? "Why, I go to Church." Wrong, people! The Church is not a building, it's the Body of Christ. Or how about this one, "You won't believe it. Somebody stole the computers by breaking into the Church." Wrong, people! The only way we the Church can be broken into is called surgery! Or how about this one, "Well, I have some bad news everybody. Last night, an arsonist came and burned down the Church"? Wrong, people! If we the Church burned down it'd be a case of spontaneous combustion, right? People, stop and think about what we're saying.

You might be thinking, "Gee whiz, Pastor Billy. Aren't you making a big deal out of nothing? I mean, so we say and do things that imply the Church is a building. So what? What's the big deal?" Big deal? I'll tell you what the big deal is. If we can't stop repeating a simple false belief that the Church is a building instead of the Body of Christ, then gee, maybe we'll start repeating other false beliefs as well. Guess what folks? It's already happening:

- 80% of Christians say the Bible teaches, "God helps those who help themselves."
- 12% say the name of Noah's wife was Joan of Arc.
- 49% say the Bible teaches that money is the root of all evil.
- 56% say the Bible proclaims the single most important task in life is taking care of one's family.
- 65% say satan does not exist.
- 29% say when Jesus lived on earth, He committed sins like everybody else.
- 55% say the Bible has errors in it.
- 25% agreed it doesn't matter what faith you follow because all paths lead to heaven.
- 49% of Pastors no longer have a Biblical worldview.
- 93% of Christians no longer have a Biblical worldview.[5]

Now folks, I'd say the American Church has a few problems with their beliefs, how about you? Why? Because if we can't stop repeating what others say and do, we're going to fall for other lies, too! If we can't even figure out who we are as believers in Christ, then how do we expect others to believe in Christ? I don't know about you, but I'd say that a pretty big deal.

Oh, but that's not all. The **2nd problem** we have is we don't say the Church is the Body of Christ. No! We say **The Church is the Body of Man**.

1 Corinthians 6:19-20 "Do you not know that your body is a temple of the Holy Spirit, who is in you, whom you have received from God? You are not your own; you were bought at a price. Therefore honor God with your body."

Now folks, according to our text, the Bible is clear. When you and me get saved, we what? We don't belong to ourselves anymore, do we? No! We were bought at a price by the blood of Jesus Christ, right? My point is this. Surely, every Christian who has ever lived knows this basic truth, right? Well, you'd think so, but that doesn't seem to be the case. Why? Because if you listen to most Christians talk, you'd think they still belonged to themselves. They still act like they're the masters of their destiny.

So, why in the world would Christians think we belong to ourselves instead of Christ? Hey, great question. I'm glad you asked. The **1st reason** is because **We Repeat what Society Says**.

People, whether you realize it or not, we live in a society that absolutely hates and utterly detests the thought that we do not belong to ourselves. Why, to say anything else is not only a sign of weakness, but a societal blasphemy. Everywhere we turn it's this attitude that life's all about you. You are your own person. You can do whatever you want. You have to love yourself. You are the center of the universe; the only person that matters in life. It's all about you, you, you! People, the point is this. If we're not careful, we'll start repeating this self-centered lie of society in what we say as Christians.

For instance, how many times have you heard Christians say something like this, "Gee, **I** wonder what God wants **me** to do with **my** life," or "**I** sure need a change in **my** life," or "**I**'m so glad **I** asked Jesus into **my** life." Excuse me? What did the Bible say? This is not our life. Are you kidding? We've been bought at a price. We don't belong to us, we belong to Christ!

Oh, but that's not all. The **2ⁿᵈ reason** we think we belong to ourselves instead of Christ is because **We Repeat what Society Sings**.

People, it's bad enough we don't pay attention to what society says and how it influences us, but we don't even pay attention to the songs they sing. For instance, how many of you guys have ever sang this song, "**Three blind mice**, see how they run! They all ran after the farmer's wife who cut off their tails with a carving knife. Did you ever see such a sight in your life as three blind mice?" Great song, right? I don't think so! Have you ever stopped to think about what were singing? It's actually a gruesome story about murder. The "farmer's wife" was Queen Mary I of England who got mad at three guys and she killed them. But, not with a carving knife, just burned at the stake.[6] Hey, great song, huh?

Oh, but that's not all. How about this one? "**Ring around the rosies**, pocket full of posies, ashes, ashes, we all fall down!" Great song right? I don't think so! It's actually a song about a person dying from the Black Plague! As it turns out, a ring around the rosies spoke of a rosy rash which was the first symptom of the plague. A pocket full of posies were carried to sweeten the air from the stench of death. Then the person would start coughing up flecks of dried blood from their lungs which looked like ashes, ashes! In the final stage they'd all fall down to do what? Die![7] Wow! What songs to teach to our kids, huh?

People, the point is this. If we're not careful, we'll start repeating the self-centered lies of society not only in what we say, but in what we sing! For instance, how many of you ever sang songs like this, "**In my life** be glorified," or even "Change **my heart**, oh God," or "**My life** is in you Lord." Excuse me? What did the Bible say? This is not our life. Are you kidding? We've been bought at a price. We don't belong to us, we belong to Christ!

You might be thinking, "Gee whiz, Pastor Billy. Aren't you making a mountain out of a molehill? Okay, so we say things and sing songs that imply we belong to ourselves. So what? What's the big deal?" Big deal? I'll tell you what the big deal is. If we can't stop repeating the simple false behavior that our lives belong to us instead of Jesus, then gee, maybe we'll start repeating other false behaviors as well. Well, guess what folks? It's already happening:

- 47% don't have a commitment to the Christian faith as a top priority.
- 58% don't have being active in a local church as one of their top goals in life.
- 42% believe that it is more important to achieve success or win acceptance from other people than to please God.
- 35% of Christians say that to get by in life these days, sometimes you have to bend the rules for your own benefit.
- 50% of Christians say there is no absolute truth.
- 33% of Christians say homosexuality is okay.
- 39% of Christians say its okay for couples to live together before marriage.
- Christians are now more likely than non-Christians to get divorced (27% vs. 24%).
- 49% of Christians don't have a problem with the distribution of pornography.
- 64% of Christians say it's okay to be a Christian and a witch.[8]

Now, folks, I'd say the American Church has got a few problems with their behavior, how about you? Why? Because if we can't stop repeating what society says and sings, we're going to start doing the very same things. The problem is when people come to us looking for Jesus, they won't be able to find Him, like with this girl. A high school girl wrote the following letter to a friend:

"I attended your Church service yesterday. Although you had invited me, you were not there. I looked for you hoping to sit with you but, I sat alone. As a stranger I wanted to sit near the back, but those rows were all packed with regular attendees.

So, an usher took me to the front. I felt as though I was on parade. During the singing of the hymns I was surprised to note that some of the Church people weren't singing. Between their sighs and yawns, they just stared into space.

Three of the kids that I had respected on campus were whispering to one another throughout the whole service. Another girl was giggling. I really didn't expect that in your Church service.

The Pastor's sermon was very interesting, although some members didn't seem to think so. They looked bored and restless. One kept smiling at someone in the congregation. There were several people who left and then came back during the sermon. I thought, 'How rude!'

I could hear the constant shuffling of feet and doors opening and closing as the Pastor spoke about the reality of faith. The message got to me and I made up my mind to speak to someone about it after the service. But utter chaos reigned after the benediction.

I said 'good morning' to one couple, but their response was less than cordial. I looked for some teens with whom I could discuss the sermon, but they were all huddled in a corner talking about the newest music group.

My parents don't go to Church services. I came alone yesterday hoping to find a place to truly worship and feel some love. I'm sorry, but I didn't find it in your congregation. And I won't be back."[9]

Now, gee folks, I'd say that Church wasn't doing a very good job of being the Body of Christ, how about you? I mean, it almost appeared like they'd totally forgotten who they were. And what was it doing? It not only affected their walk with Christ, but it kept that girl from coming to Christ!

People, if we can't stop playing Church instead of being the Church then maybe it's time to get out of the Church. Why? Because being a Christian is not a game. What we say and do literally affects the eternal destiny of people around us. Therefore, it's high time we get rid of our practical amnesia. We have to remember who we are! People, the Church is not a building and it doesn't belong to itself. People, the Church is a Body. It's **The Body of Jesus Christ!**

Chapter Two

A Body of Brides

Recently there was a Church that had to look for a new Pastor, so guess what they did? Hey, that's right! They called in the **Pastoral Search Committee** to do their job, right? Of course! Folks, not that there's anything wrong with a search committee, but wait till you see this Church's criteria for picking a Pastor. Here are some of the guys they looked at but decided for various reasons to pass on.

- **Noah:** He has 120 years of preaching experience, but no converts.

- **Moses:** He stutters and his former congregation says he loses his temper over trivial things.

- **Abraham:** He took off to Egypt during hard times. We heard that he got into trouble with the authorities and then tried to lie his way out.

- **David:** He is of an unacceptable moral character. He might have been considered for minister of music had he not 'fallen.'

- **Solomon:** He has a reputation for wisdom, but fails to practice what he preaches.

- **Elijah:** He proved to be inconsistent and is known to fold under pressure.

- **Hosea:** His family life is in a shambles. He's divorced and then got remarried to a prostitute.

- **Jeremiah:** He is too emotional, loud and an alarmist. Some say he is a real 'pain in the neck.'

- **Amos:** He does come from a farming background, but he'd be better off picking figs.

- **John:** He says he is a Baptist, but he lacks tact and dresses like a hippie. He wouldn't feel comfortable at a potluck supper.

- **Peter:** He has a bad temper, and was heard to even have denied Christ publicly.

- **Paul:** We found him to lack tact. In fact, he's too harsh and his appearance is contemptible. Besides, he preaches too long.

- **Timothy:** He has potential, but he's much too young for the position.

- **Jesus:** He tends to offend Church members with his preaching and He's too controversial. In fact, He even offended the search committee with his pointed questions.

- But, we did find one guy. He seemed to be very practical, co-operative, good with money, cares for the poor, and dresses well. So, we all agreed that he's just the man we're looking for to be our Senior Pastor. His name? **Judas Iscariot!**[1]

Now, how many of you guys can appreciate the saying, "For God so loved the world that He did not send a committee"? Wow! What was the problem there? That Church had no idea what they were doing, right?

But folks, believe it or not, do you know many Churches today not only have no idea what they're doing, but get this, they don't even know who they are? Why? Because they're acting like they have practical amnesia!

Oh, we say we know who the Church is, but half the time, with our lips and with our lives, we act like we've forgotten who we are. It's not only detrimental in our walk with Christ. It keeps others from believing in Christ. Therefore, to avoid this atrocity of Christians acting like they have practical amnesia by not knowing who they are, we're going to continue our study from the Word of God on the people of God entitled, "**The Character of the Church.**"

In the last chapter we saw the first thing we need to know about the Church if we're going to stop acting like we have practical amnesia is that The Church is the Body of Christ. There we saw the American Church no longer calls itself the Body of Christ. No! Apparently that's too simple. They call the Church a Building or the Body of Man and imply that we belong to us instead of Jesus, which is not only unbiblical, it's blasphemous! Jesus Christ is the Head or Chief Authority over not just the entire universe but the Church, which means He calls the shots, He tells us what to do, not the other way around!

People, believe it or not, that's not the only thing we need to know if we're going to stop acting like we have practical amnesia. The **second thing** we need to know about the Church is that **The Church is the Bride of Christ.** But hey, don't take my word for it. Let's listen to God's:

Ephesians 5:25-32 "Husbands, love your wives, just as Christ loved the church and gave himself up for her to make her holy, cleansing her by the washing with water through the word, and to present her to himself as a radiant church, without stain or wrinkle or any other blemish, but holy and blameless. In this same way, husbands ought to love their wives as their own bodies. He who loves his wife loves himself. After all, no one ever hated his own body, but he feeds and cares for it, just as Christ does the church – for we are members of his body. For this reason a man will leave his father and mother and be united to his wife, and the two will become one flesh. This is a profound mystery – but I am talking about Christ and the church."

Now folks, according to the text, the Bible is clear. We the Church are not only members of the Body of Christ, but we're what? We're the wife or Bride of Christ, right? Here's my point. Surely, we all know that, right? I mean, surely every Christian who has ever lived knows that we're the Bride of Christ, right? Well, you'd think so, but we have some problems. Why? Because if you look at the behavior of most Christians it appears that we don't have a beautiful bride-like relationship with Christ. No! We have a dry stale boring religion with Christ!

So, why in the world would Christians think we have a religion with Christ instead of a relationship? Hey, great question. I'm glad you asked. It's pretty simple. The **first reason** we think we have a religion with Christ instead of a relationship is because **We've Forgotten the Words of Christ**. People, I don't know if you've noticed this or not, but throughout the Gospels, Jesus went to great lengths to make sure we knew the purpose of His Coming. And it wasn't to start a new religion. How do I know? Because with His own words, Jesus declared He'd come for a beautiful intimate relationship with people, just like with a bride. How? By comparing our relationship with Him to the Seven Phases of a Jewish Marriage Ceremony.[2]

So, how are these Seven Phases of a Jewish Marriage Ceremony speaking of God's desire for a relationship and not a religion? Hey, great question. I'm glad you asked. The **first phase** is **the "Shiddukhin" or the "Match."** You see, unlike today, Jewish marriages were arranged by the fathers. What the father would do is get a person do be the "matchmaker" and go find a bride for the son. Gee folks, guess what? That's exactly what the Bible says Jesus did for you and me.

John 15:16 "You did not choose Me, but I chose you..."

John 6:37;44 "All that the Father gives me will come to me…No one can come to me unless the Father who sent me draws him."

Now folks, I'd say that's pretty interesting, how about you? In fact, if you keep thinking about it, you'll see that's exactly what we're doing when we get saved. We're accepting Jesus' love proposal to be "matched" or married to Him forever.

Oh, but that's not all. The **second phase** in a Jewish marriage ceremony was called the "**Mohar**" or the "**Bride Price**." Right after the "match" was made, a mohar or bride price was hashed out between both parties over the value of the Bride. Gee folks, guess what? That's exactly what the Bible says Jesus did for you and me. In fact, the price He paid was extremely high!

1 Corinthians 6:20 "You are not your own. For you have been bought with a price..."

1 Peter 1:18 "Knowing that your were not redeemed with perishable things...but with precious blood...the blood of Christ."

Now folks, I'd say that's a pretty high bride price, don't you think? And if Jesus paid that big of a price for us, then I'd say He must love us an awful lot, how about you?

Oh, but that's not all. The **third phase** in a Jewish marriage ceremony was called the "**Mattan**" or the "**love gifts**." Now in this phase, the groom would offer the bride gifts even though he didn't have to. He simply did it as an expression of his love for her. Gee, guess what folks? That's exactly what the Bible said Jesus did for you and me. He gave us some awesome love gifts! Check it out for yourself:

ETERNAL LIFE: **John 10:27-28** "My sheep hear My voice and I know them, and they follow Me; and I give eternal life to them, and they shall never perish; and no one shall snatch them out of My hand."

PEACE: **John 14:27** "Peace I leave with you; My peace I give to you..."

FORGIVENESS: **1 John 1:9** "If we confess our sins, He is faithful and just and will forgive us our sins and purify us from all unrighteousness."

JOY: **John 15:11** "I have told you this so that my joy may be in you and that your joy may be complete."

Now folks, I'd say those are some pretty awesome "love gifts," how about you? What you need to keep in mind is that these "love gifts" are voluntary. Jesus didn't have to give them. Therefore, I'd say He sure must love us an awful lot, how about you?

Oh, but that's not all. The **fourth phase** in a Jewish marriage ceremony was called the "**Shiluhim**" or the "**dowry**." Now in this phase, the Father of the bride would give her gifts. The purpose of these gifts was to help equip her for her new life with the groom. Gee, guess what folks? That's exactly what the Bible says God the Father has done for you and me. Listen to how He equipped us.

THE SPIRIT TO LIVE FOR HIM: **John 14:16-17** "And I will ask the Father and He will give you another Helper…that is the Spirit of truth."

SPIRITUAL GIFTS TO SERVE HIM: **Romans 12:6** "We have different gifts, according to the grace given us."

AN ENGAGEMENT RING TO REMEMBER HIM: **2 Corinthians 1:21-22** "Now He who established us with you in Christ and anointed us is God, who also sealed us and gave us the Spirit in our hearts as a pledge."

Now folks, the word "pledge" here is actually the Greek word for "engagement ring." People, the Bible says that God gives us the Holy Spirit as a reminder that one day we'll be with Him forever, just like the reminder of an engagement ring. What a gift, huh?

Oh, but that's not all. The **fifth phase** in a Jewish marriage ceremony was called the "**Ketubah**" or the "**marriage contract**." Now in this phase, the marriage was legally formalized by a written marriage contract called the ketubah. It recorded the bride price, the promises of the groom, and the rights of the bride. Gee, guess what folks? That's exactly what the Bible says God has done for you and me. How? By giving us the New Contract or covenant stated by Jesus Himself.

1 Corinthians 11:25 "In the same way He took the cup also after supper, saying, 'This cup is the new covenant in My blood; do this, as often as you drink it, in remembrance of Me."

People, whether you realize it or not, every time we take communion, it's a reminder of our marriage contract with Jesus. If Jesus signed our marriage contract with His own blood then gee I'd say it's pretty secure, how about you?

Oh, but that's not all. The **sixth phase** in a Jewish marriage ceremony was called the "**kiddushin**" or the "**betrothal**." It was here that after the marriage contract was signed the couple became what was called betrothed. Even though this meant they were legally married, they still didn't live together. Why? Because they still had to go and make preparations for their new life together. For instance, the groom had to go back to his father's house and start building an addition to the house called the bridal chamber. It was here that they would consummate their marriage and settle down and live together as a family. Gee, guess what folks? That's exactly what the Bible says Jesus is doing right now for you and me.

John 14:2-3 "In My Father's house are many dwelling places; if it were not so, I would have told you; for I go to prepare a place for you. And if I go and prepare a place for you, I will come again, and receive you to Myself; that where I am, there you may be also."

Now folks, if God took six days to create the heavens and the earth in all its majesty, then can you imagine how incredible our bridal chamber is if Jesus' been working on it for two thousand years?

Oh, but that's not all. The **seventh and final stage** in the Jewish wedding ceremony was the "**nissuin**" or "**the taking**." Now once the chamber was completed, the Father would inspect it and tell the son, "Okay, go get your bride." The neat romantic thing about this was the Jewish bride had no idea when he was coming. It could be at anytime. Therefore, she always had to be ready for his sudden arrival. When he did arrive, he would take or abduct her and whisk her away to the Father's house. Gee, guess what folks? That's exactly what the Bible says we need to be ready for! Why? Because Jesus could come at any moment and abduct us, His bride, the Church.

1 Thessalonians 4:16,17 "For the Lord Himself will descend from heaven with a shout...Then we who are alive and remain shall be caught up together with them in the clouds to meet the Lord in the air, and thus we shall always be with the Lord."

Now folks, I don't know if you know this or not, but the words "caught up" is where we get our word 'rapture' from. What it literally means is a "catching or snatching away" just like an abduction. Hmmm. Now, I'd think after two thousand years, Jesus must be getting close to finishing that Bridal Chamber, right? Therefore, wouldn't it make sense to make sure we're ready to go?

People the bigger point is this. It's obvious by the Words of Christ that He intended for us to have a beautiful bride-like relationship with Him, right? Therefore, where does the American Church get off treating our relationship with Christ as a religion? I mean do we really think He likes us twisting His words? I don't think so, folks. Why? Because you should listen to what He said to the religious people of His day. Maybe you've heard of them. They were called the Pharisees. Here's what He called them to their face in Matthew chapter twenty-three. He called them a bunch of blind men, blind fools, blind guides, brood of vipers, band of murderers, bag of dead people's bones and a bunch hypocrites! Gee whiz folks, it doesn't seem that Jesus was too pleased with the Pharisees. Why? Because they twisted and perverted what He said, what He had worked so hard for! They tried to take the beautiful bride-like relationship with God and turn it into a dry, stale, stupid, and boring religion.

People, the point is this. If Jesus didn't like it then, then how do you think He likes it today? Therefore, I'd say the American Church's treatment of our relationship with God as a religion, really is a big deal, how about you?

Oh, but that's not all. The **second reason** why we think we have a religion with Christ instead of a relationship is because **We've Forgotten the Works of Christ**.

Romans 5:6,8 "You see, at just the right time, when we were still powerless, Christ died for the ungodly. But God demonstrates his own love for us in this: While we were still sinners, Christ died for us."

Now folks, according to our text, the Bible is clear. When Jesus died on the cross, He didn't do it for his best buddies, did He? No! He did it for who? The ungodly, the sinners, you and me, right? So, here's my question: How many of you think Jesus went through all that pain and torture on the cross just so he could start a brand new religion and build giant buildings across the world? No, of course not, right? It was obvious that He did that work on the cross for a relationship, right?

Here's my point. Surely every Christian who has ever lived knows that Jesus died on the cross for a relationship, right? Well, you'd think so, but that doesn't seem to be the case. Why? Because if you listen to most Christians talk, you'd think Jesus died so we could have some sort of religious country club where we tell each other how wonderful we are because we do wonderful religious things.

So, why in the world would we do this? Why do Christians think Jesus' work on the cross was for a religion instead of a relationship? Hey, great question. I'm glad you asked. It's pretty simple. The main reason we do it is because we not only treat His work on the cross like a Religion but We Celebrate it like a Religion. People, whether you realize it or not, one of the biggest atrocities of the American Church is to not only in treating our relationship with God as a religion, but get this, we even make it an annual event! How? By the way we celebrate Resurrection Day, or what many have now relabeled as Easter! People, hello! Celebrating Resurrection Day is not bad! Praise God we can celebrate the day that Jesus raised from the dead for our sins, right? That should be a time of celebration. People, the problem is the way we celebrate it. Let's be honest. We've been tricked by our culture into twisting and perverting the work of Christ on the cross. How do I know? Because Resurrection Day is no longer about the provision for sin that Jesus has made. No! It's about an egg-laying chocolate-covered fuzzy-bunny parade!

And to show you how horrible this behavior is to the work of Christ, let's compare what society says about this time of celebration is all about versus what the Savior says. You see, if you asked the average person what Resurrection Day is all about would they would not say it's all about getting a new bonnet for our head? Of course! But doesn't the Bible say it's all about Jesus being given a crown of thorns on His head? Or if you asked the average person today what Resurrection Day is all about would they not say it's all about getting a big ol' bag of candy? Of course! But doesn't the Bible say it's about Jesus bearing the cross for the sins of humanity? Or if you asked the average person today what Resurrection Day is all about would they not say that it's about getting a big giant bunny drenched with chocolate? Of course! But doesn't the Bible say it's about Jesus on the cross dripping with blood for all our sins? Therefore, in light of this behavior, I'd say God's probably not too pleased with what we've done with Resurrection Day, how about you?

You might be thinking, "Gee whiz, Pastor Billy. Aren't you making a mountain out of a molehill? Okay, so we treat our relationship with God like a religion and we even celebrate it like one. So what? What's the big deal?" Big deal? I'll tell you what the big deal is. Treating our relationship with God as a religion not only effects our walk with Christ, it spreads to others and kills their chances of believing in Christ, like with this story:

"In the 1500's, there was a cabin boy named Juan. He was an employee of the Panfile Narvaez Fleet. And like all boys of his age, Juan decided to

break the rules and jump ship and explore the new territory the ship discovered on the Coast of Mexico.

And this may have sounded innocent enough, but the only problem was, Juan was infected with the smallpox virus. Because of his one act of disobedience, Juan's deadly influential presence was responsible for the deaths of three million Indians. "[3]

Now folks, I'd that one act of disobedience was just a little bit costly, how about you? Here's my point! How many millions of people have been turned off to Christ because we the Church have infected them with a religious disease! How many of those people have died and gone to hell because we were too busy playing Church instead of being the Church?

People of God, this is why being a Christian is not a game. What we say and do affects the eternal destiny of people around us. Therefore, it's high time we get rid of our practical amnesia. We have to remember who we are! People we don't have a religion with God. We have a relationship with God. Why? Because the Church is a Body. It's **A Body of Brides**!

Chapter Three

A Body of One

"It was called "the greatest scab and cancer on the face of Christianity in two thousand years of Church history;" brought on by a class action suit on behalf of more than 160,000 onetime believers who contributed as much as $7,000 each in a ministry that over the years amassed an empire worth $158 million dollars.

However, this so-called Christian ministry didn't appear to be very wise with the use of this money. For instance, one time they spent more than $100 on a purchase of cinnamon rolls. Not eat them, but just so they could smell them in their hotel room.

Not only that, they had a regular practice of spending over $100,000 on a private jet just to fly their clothing across the country. Then they spent $60,000 in gold-plated bathroom fixtures and thousands of dollars on an air-conditioned dog house that tunred out to be too noisy for the dog so he never even slept in it.

On top of that, this husband and wife duo received annual salaries of $200,000 each and even awarded themselves over four million dollars in *bonuses. Because of this, they owned a six mansions, lots of luxury cars and had forty-seven separate bank accounts.*

And of course I'm talking about the Church scandal of Jim and Tammy Faye Bakker."[1]

Now, how many of you guys after that scandal could never look at eyelashes the same again? Folks, believe it or not, big creepy eyelashes weren't the only scary things about that scandal. Get this. The creepiest thing was how it forever changed overnight the way people viewed the American Church. I mean, correct me if I'm wrong but ever since that scandal, does not your average person today think the Church is full of nothing but weird greedy hypocrites who only want to swindle you out of your money, right? Folks, believe it or not, as creepy as that scandal was, do you know there's one even bigger than that. It's not only being repeated every single day, but it's being repeated by millions of Christians all at the same time. Can anybody guess what it is? Hey, that's right! It's when Christians act like they have practical amnesia!

Oh, we say we know who we are as the Church, but half the time, with our lips and with our lives, we act like we've forgotten who we are. It's not only detrimental in our walk with Christ. It keeps others from believing in Christ. Therefore, to avoid this atrocity of Christians living like they have practical amnesia by not knowing who they are, we're going to continue our study from the Word of God on the people of God entitled, **"The Character of the Church."**

We've already seen the first thing we need to know about the Church if we're going to stop acting like we have practical amnesia is that the Church is the Body of Christ. In the last chapter we saw the second thing we need to know is that the Church is a Body of Brides. There we saw how the American Church no longer acts like we have a beautiful loving intimate bride-like relationship with Christ. No! We act like we have a dry, stale, stupid, and boring religion with Christ. Why? Because we not only treat it like one, we celebrate it like one!

People, believe it or not, do you know that's not the only thing we need to know about the Church if we're going to stop acting like we have practical amnesia? The **third thing** we need to know is **The Church is a Body of One**. But hey, don't take my word for it. Let's listen to God's:

Ephesians 4:1-6 "As a prisoner for the Lord, then, I urge you to live a life worthy of the calling you have received. Be completely humble and gentle; be patient, bearing with one another in love. Make every effort to keep the unity of the Spirit through the bond of peace. There is one body and one Spirit – just as you were called to one hope when you were called – one Lord, one faith, one baptism; one God and Father of all, who is over all and through all and in all."

Now folks, according to our text, the Bible is clear. We the Church are made up of many different "bodies" physically but spiritually in the eyes of God we're considered what? A Body of One. Why? Because our unity is not achieved on the basis of external appearances but because of an internal spiritual truth. That is, we all have one faith, one Lord, one baptism, one hope, one God, which makes us all what? One right? Here's my point. Surely, we all know that, right? I mean, surely every Christian who has ever lived knows that the Church is a Body of One, right? Well, you'd think so, but we have some problems. Why? Because if you look at most Churches it doesn't look like we have a unified bond of peace with each other. Are you kidding? It looks like we have a divided wall of separation with each other!

So, why in the world would Christians behave so divisive when the Bible says we're already unified? Hey, great question. I'm glad you asked. It's pretty simple. The **first reason** we behave so divisive is because **We Give in to Spiritual Favoritism**.

1 Corinthians 3:1,3,4 "Dear brothers and sisters, when I was with you I couldn't talk to you as I would to mature Christians. I had to talk as though you belonged to this world. You are acting like people who don't belong to the Lord. When one of you says, 'I am a follower of Paul,' and another says, 'I prefer Apollos,' aren't you acting like those who are not Christians?"

Now folks, according to our text, the Bible is clear. One of the major issues Paul had to keep confronting over and over again with the Corinthian believers was what? Divisions in the Church. Why? Because they were being selective with who they were going to hang out with. They were giving into favoritism, right? Oh, you can hear them now, "Why, I'm only going to hang out with Paul! After all, he comes from a big city like me." "Oh yeah! Well, I'm only going to hang out with Apollos. He's more down to earth and after all, he's one of the local boys."

People, the point is this. Surely the American Church would never do something like that, right? I mean, surely that was a mistake that only the Corinthians did, right? People, Are you kidding? If you believe that, I've got a chicken ranch in Alaska to sell you! Come on, man! Let's be honest. Giving into favoritism was not only a problem with the Corinthian Church. It's a huge problem with the American Church! I mean, you've been there. You go into the average Church service today and what do you see? You don't see the Family of God mingling together in a blessed unity. No! You see, Christian cliques separating each other week after week!

You might be thinking, "So what? So I only hang out with the same people every week. What's the big deal?" Big deal? I'll tell you what the big deal is. What did the text say? When Christians act like this, they're acting like what? Like immature babies, right? In fact, they're acting like they're not even Christians at all! Why? Because people we're a Body of One! We're the unified Family of God. Because of that there's no stinkin' reason for a Christian to ever have to feel like an outsider. In fact, the Bible says we need to go out of our way to make sure all believers feel like they fit in, just like these boys did:

"Ian was a fifth grade boy in Oceanside, California who one day got the news that he had cancer. And so having no choice in the matter, he immediately had to begin chemotherapy.

And if that wasn't bad enough, Ian faced the reality of having his hair fall out in clumps so he had to shave his head. And this of course, as you can imagine, wasn't a very cool thing to have to do for a fifth grader.

But then that's when one of Ian's classmates, Kyle Hanslik, got an idea. He said, 'If all of us boys in the fifth grade have our heads shaved, then nobody will know who's who. They won't know who has cancer, and who doesn't.'

So Kyle, and the rest of the fifth grade boys, made their manly decision. All thirteen went to the barbershop and shaved their heads too. Why? Because as Kyle said, 'The last thing Ian needs now is to feel like he doesn't fit in.'"[2]

Now folks, I'd say those boys understood the importance of needing to fit in somewhere, how about you? Exactly! Here's my question. Why is it a group of fifth grade boys can get it, but the American Church can't? Why is it that ten year olds can sacrifice and shave their heads for a boy with cancer, but we can't even shake the hand of a fellow Christian?

People of God, there is no excuse for a Christian to ever feel like an outsider when they go to Church services. Why? Because our God-given unity ensures that no matter who we are, we should always have a place to fit in! People, I'm telling you, the longer we give into favoritism, we'll not only cease to be a unified Body of One, but we'll actually turn into a divided **Bunch of Snobs**.

Oh, but that's not all. The **second reason** we behave so divisive is because **We Give into Spiritual Elitism**.

Acts 2:44,46,47 "And all the believers met together in one place and shared everything they had. They worshiped together at the Temple each day, met in homes for the Lord's Supper, and shared their meals with great joy and generosity. And each day the Lord added to their fellowship those who were being saved."

Now folks, according to our text, the Bible is clear. One of the reasons why the early Church experienced so much growth was because of what? They not only lived in harmony with each other in Church services, but get this. They carried that harmony right into their homes. I mean, can you believe that? Christians hanging out with each other outside of Church services? When people came to check out this unified behavior what did the Church do? Well, apparently they welcomed them with open arms because God did what? He was adding new people every single day, right?

People, the point is this. Surely the American Church does the same thing, right? I mean, surely we too open our arms wide to newcomers, right? People, Are you kidding? If you believe that, I've got a box of frozen chicken lips to sell you as well! Come on man! Let's be honest. Giving into elitism is a huge problem with the American Church! I mean, you've been there. You go into the average Church service today and what do you see? You don't see the Family of God excited to see new people coming to praise God Most High. No! You see, them giving visitors the ol' cold shoulder and the deadly evil eye!

You might be thinking, "So what? So I'm not the warmest welcome wagon to every new person that walks through the door. In fact, I could care less if any new people walk through that door. What's the big deal?" Big deal? I'll tell you what the big deal is. People, we are a Body of One! We're the unified Family of God. Because of that there's no reason for a newcomer to ever feel like an outsider. Why? Because has it ever occurred to you that God might want to have other children in His Family besides you and me? Hello! People, that's precisely why the Bible says we need to go out of our way to make sure all newcomers get a warm welcome, no matter who they are, like this man did:

"One Sunday, a college student named Mike decided to go to Church services across the street from his dorm. So being a college student and all, he showed up in his regular attire, which included torn jeans, a T-shirt, some pretty wild looking hair, and no shoes.

When he got there, not only had the service already started but the sanctuary was completely packed and he couldn't find a seat. But he didn't want to give up, so he just started down the aisle getting closer and closer to the pulpit.

Well by now, all eyes were on him and the congregation was getting very uncomfortable with his presence. And since Mike still couldn't find a seat, he just squatted right down on the carpet in front of the pulpit.

Well, by now the people are really uptight, and the tension in the air is thick. And it was about this time that a deacon sitting in the back of the Sanctuary, got up out of his pew and headed towards the boy. He was a very dignified man in his eighties and wore an elegant three-piece suit.

As he was approaching the boy, the congregation was saying to themselves, 'You can't blame him for what he's going to do. How can you expect a man of his age and stature let some college kid sit on the floor?'

As the deacon finally made it to where Mike was sitting, the whole congregation was completely silent. You could have heard a pin drop. But then suddenly, with great difficulty because of his age, the deacon lowered himself and sat right down next to Mike so he wouldn't have to worship God alone.

At this the minister simply said, 'What I am about to preach, you will never remember. But what you have just seen, you will never forget.'"[3]

Now folks, I'd say that deacon did a pretty good job of welcoming that newcomer, how about you? Here's my question. Why is it an eighty year old man can get it, but the American Church can't? Why is it that an old man can sacrifice his own comfort zone and sit on the floor with a strange boy, but we can't even share a pew with a stranger?

People of God, there is no excuse for a newcomer to ever feel like an outsider when they go to Church services. Why? Because God wants us to welcome others no matter who they are just like He did with you and me. People, I'm telling you, the longer we give into elitism, we not only cease to be a unified Body of One, but we actually turn into a divided **Bunch of Bigots**.

Oh, but that's not all. The **third reason** we behave divisive is because **We Give into Spiritual Racism**.

Galatians 3:26,28 "So you are all children of God through faith in Christ Jesus. There is no longer Jew or Gentile, slave or free, male or female. For you are all Christians – you are one in Christ Jesus."

Now folks, according to our text, the Bible is clear. One of the most revolutionary truths you will never find in this world is that the moment you get saved, all gender, all racial, all ethnic barriers are what? They're forever removed, right? Therefore, the opportunity to become a part of God's family is opened to who? To anyone and everyone, right?

The point is this. Surely the American Church knows this, right? I mean, surely we all know that red or yellow or black or white, they're all precious in Jesus' sight, right? People, Are you kidding? Giving into racism is a huge problem with the American Church! I mean, you've been there. You go into the average Church service today and what do you see? You don't see the Family of God advancing God's love to all kinds of people. No! You see, them retreating behind stained glass windows and big ol' steeples.

You might be thinking, "So what? So I don't reach out to different people for Christ. In fact, I could care less about reaching anyone. What's the big deal?" Big deal? I'll tell you what the big deal is. People, we are a Body of One! We're the unified Family of God. Because of that there's no reason for anyone to ever feel like an outsider. Why? Because has it ever occurred to you that God might want to have all kinds of different children in His Family besides you and me? Hello! People, that's precisely why the Bible says we need to go out of our way to make sure everyone gets an opportunity to hear the gospel, like this Church did. The following is about a Church in North Carolina that learned to share God's love to anyone and everyone during the sixties in the segregated South. However, it wasn't always that way. Listen to what they had to go through before they started behaving as a Body of One:

"In the fifties, a friend of mine named Clarence Thomas, was once invited to go to a Church service in North Carolina. This was prior to the civil rights movement in the sixties and segregation was still very much prevalent. But much to his surprise, when he got there, he discovered that the congregation was totally integrated, fifty-fifty, black and white. And given the times, he was obviously surprised at this, especially in North Carolina where racism was so extreme.

So when the service was over he asked the ol' hillbilly Preacher there 'How'd you get this way?'

The ol' hillbilly Preacher said, 'What way?'

Clarence responded, 'You know, black people, white people together. How did this happen?'

The Preacher began his story. 'I'll tell you how we got this way. You see, we were a small Church and had about twenty members.' (Well, Clarence said there were hundreds and hundreds in the congregation that night.)

The preacher continued. 'And one day our Preacher died and we couldn't get a new Preacher no how. So after two or three months I went to the deacons and told them that if they couldn't get a Preacher that I'd be the Preacher. So they let me preach.

I got up there the next Sunday and I opened up my Bible and put my finger down (that's the way they do it back there in the hills) and it landed on a verse. It said, 'In Christ there is neither Jew nor Greek, bond nor free, male nor female, that everybody's one in Christ Jesus.'

I told them that the Church, when the Church is a true Church, that they don't know any of these racial divisions, they don't know any of these ethnic divisions, that everybody's one in the Church of Jesus Christ. I preached that to them. After the service was over, the deacons called me in the back room. They told me they didn't want to hear that kind of preaching no more.'

Clarence said, 'Well what did you do then?'

The ol' hillbilly Preacher said, 'I FIRED them deacons!' (Well, if a deacon's not going to 'deac' and and elder's not going to 'eld,' you got to fire them.)

Clarence said, 'How come they didn't fire you?'

The Preacher said, 'Because they never hired me! And once I found out what bothered those people, I gave it to them every week!' (Do you know Preacher's like that? Once they find out what bothers you, they put the knife in at the same spot every time and turn it?)

Clarence said, 'Did they put up with it?'

The ol' hillbilly said, 'I preached that Church down to four!' (You know, sometimes people, revival begins not when you get a lot of new people into the Church. Sometimes revival begins when what? When you get a lot of the old people out of the Church.)

Then Clarence said, 'Well, what happened then?'

The Preacher said, 'Well from then on we wouldn't let anybody in that Church unless they really loved Jesus.'

Clarence said, 'How can you tell if people really love Jesus?'

The Preacher said, 'Well, when people love Jesus, they love each other no matter who the other person is.'"

Now folks, I'd say that Church was doing a real good job of being a Body of One, how about you? Here's my question. Why is it that an ol' hillbilly preacher can get it, but the American Church can't? Why is it that a Church in the South is willing to share God's love with anyone and everyone but the rest of us won't?

People, we don't need a revival in America. We need revival in the American Church! Why? Because apparently we can't stop playing Church instead of being the Church long enough for revival to take place! People, that's why being a Christian is not a game. What we say and do affects the eternal destiny of people around us. Therefore, it's high time we get rid of our practical amnesia. We have to remember who we are! We're not a bunch of snobs or bigots and we're not a bunch of racists. The Church is a Body. **A Body of One**!

Chapter Four

A Body of Hope

Hey, how many of you guys ever played that game "Twenty Questions"? You know, where you share some facts and information about somebody and you have to guess who it is? Well hey, that's right! Since we're Christians and we like to have fun, right? We're going to play our own version of "Twenty Questions," only we're going to keep it to ten. Let's see if you can guess who this person is.

1. This person has no Biblical or theological training yet addresses a congregation of 12,000 every week.

2. His "ministry" takes in over $100 million a year, which allows him to maintain a $3.5 million home, spend $8,000 on airline fares and stay in $2,000 a night hotel rooms.

3. He prophesied that Fidel Castro would die in the 1990's.

4. He prophesied that God would destroy the homosexual community in America by fire in 1994-95.

5. He prophesied that the leader of Syria would make a peace treaty with Israel in the year 2000 but when the leader died he said it was not God's plan after all.

6. He says that Jesus is "physically" appearing to Muslims right now.

7. He said Jesus would "physically" appear in Nairobi, Kenya.

8. He said Jesus would "physically" appear at one of his meetings, possibly in Nashville.

9. He said that Adam could fly like a bird, swim underwater like a fish, and even transport himself to the moon.

10. And finally, this so-called Christian minister said this to those who dared to criticize him, "I've looked for one verse in the Bible - I just can't seem to find it - one verse that said if you don't like them, kill them...I wish God would give me a Holy Ghost machine gun - I'll blow your head off!"

11. Who is this person? Why it's none other than television evangelist, BENNY HINN![1]

Now, how many of you guys would say that so-called Christian evangelist probably isn't the best representative of Christianity? But folks, believe it or not, do you know there's an even worse representation than that? And get this, it's not being done just by one man. It's being done by millions of Christians all at the same time. Can anybody guess who it is? Hey, that's right! It's when Christians act like they have practical amnesia!

Oh, we say we know who we are as the Church, but half the time, with our lips and with our lives, we act like we've forgotten who we are. It's not only detrimental in our walk with Christ. It keeps others from believing in Christ. Therefore, to avoid this atrocity of Christians living like they have practical amnesia by not knowing who they are, we're going to continue our study from the Word of God on the people of God entitled, "**The Character of the Church**."

We've already seen the first thing we need to know about the Church if we're going to stop acting like we have practical amnesia is that the Church is the Body of Christ. The second thing is that the Church is a Body of Brides. In the last chapter we saw the third thing we need to know is that the Church is a Body of One. There we saw, believe it or not, how the American Church is actually behaving divisively even though the Bible says we're already unified. Why? Because we give into favoritism, elitism, and racism. Because of that, we're not only ceasing to be a Body of One, we're actually turning into a Body of snobs and bigots. I don't think that's the kind of Church Jesus came to die for, how about you?

People, believe it or not, do you know that's not the only thing we need to know about the Church if we're going to stop acting like we have practical amnesia? The **fourth thing** we need to know is **The Church is a Body of Hope**. But hey, don't take my word for it. Let's listen to God's:

Romans 15:8-13 "For I tell you that Christ has become a servant of the Jews on behalf of God's truth, to confirm the promises made to the patriarchs so that the Gentiles may glorify God for his mercy, as it is written: Therefore I will praise you among the Gentiles; I will sing hymns to your name. Again, it says, Rejoice, O Gentiles, with his people. And again, Praise the Lord, all you Gentiles, and sing praises to him, all you peoples. And again, Isaiah says, The Root of Jesse will spring up, one who will arise to rule over the nations; the Gentiles will hope in him. May the God of hope fill you with all joy and peace as you trust in him, so that you may overflow with hope by the power of the Holy Spirit."

Now folks, according to our text, the Bible is clear. One of the main reasons why Jesus came and died on the cross was to save not only Jewish people but Gentile people for what purpose? For the glory of God, right? And one of the benefits of having God save you for His glory is not only being filled with joy and peace, but what? He fills you with hope, right? Notice is wasn't just a little hope. It's so much hope that we're literally bubbling over with it for all the world to see, right?

Here's my point. Surely, we all know that, right? I mean, surely every Christian who has ever lived knows that the Church is to be a Body of Hope, where people look at us and say, "Wow! Now there's a group of people who never get discouraged and are always full of optimism," right? Well, you'd think so, but we have some problems. Why? Because if you look at most Churches it doesn't look like we're an optimistic people bubbling with hope. Are you kidding? It looks like a pack of pessimists dangling by a rope!

So, why in the world would Christians look so hopeless when the Bible says we should be so hopeful? Hey, great question. I'm glad you asked. It's pretty simple. The **first reason** we look so hopeless is because we've forgotten we've been given a **Stable Life**.

Romans 5:1,3-4 "By faith we have been made acceptable to God. And now, because of our Lord Jesus Christ, we live at peace with God. But that's not all! We gladly suffer, because we know that suffering helps us to endure. And endurance builds character, which gives us a hope that will never disappoint us."

Now folks, according to our text, the Bible is clear. One of the most incredible things God gives us after we're saved is not only peace with Him, but what? Hope in Him, right? And since our hope is in God, it never disappoints us. Why? Because hope in God gives us the ability to have stability in all our difficulties, right?

People, the point is this. Surely the American Church knows this, right? I mean, surely no matter what we go through in life, people never see us down in the mouth or disappointed, right? People, Are you kidding? I mean, you've been there. You go into the average Church service today and what do you see? You don't see Christians enduring through difficulties coming out mighty and strong. No! You see, people who look like they just lost their house and somebody ran over their dog!

You might be thinking, "Well hey, I think you're being a little too harsh here. I mean, it's obvious you don't understand my problems! I mean, if you knew what I was going through, you'd understand why I look so hopeless half the time!" Excuse me? Maybe you should tell that to John Bunyan who was unjustly put in prison? Did he cry? Did he whine and give up hope! No people! Are you kidding? While he was in prison he wrote the Christian classic "Pilgrim's Progress" and that one book has encouraged millions of people to place their hope in God just like John did, in prison.[2]

Or maybe you should tell it to Fanny Crosby who was made blind by a Doctor's mistake? I mean, surely if anyone has a great excuse to bellyache before God it's her, right? I mean, surely she just cried and whined for the rest of her life, right? No people! God used that one Christian woman's blindness to open the hearts of millions of people. How? By writing over three thousand hymns of praise inspiring them to place their hope in God as well![3]

Or maybe you should tell it to Paul and Silas who were put in jail for the Gospel? I mean surely they were ticked off at God for allowing something like that to happen right? No people! With their backs bloody and beaten, they put their hope in God, praised Him all night long from the top of their lungs until an earthquake came set them free!

Oh, but that's still not all. Maybe you should tell it to this Christian woman. I mean, if there was ever anyone who should've given up hope it was this lady:

"One morning in Southern California, a young hopeful Christian bride of less than a year received a knock at her apartment door. Her husband had already left for work so she was a little uneasy about opening the door but she went ahead and did it anyway.

When she did, she saw a man standing in front of her that she'd never seen before. In fact, he seemed nervous, and that increased her uneasiness. But then he simply asked about the location of the manager's apartment and so she gave him the information and promptly shut the door.

But only a few minutes later, there came another knock. So the young bride, cautious, but not cautious enough, opened the door again. When she did, the long blade of the same man's knife pushed her back into the room. Then he locked the door, closed the drapes, and told her to completely disrobe.

But at that very fearful moment, this young Christian woman looked straight into the face of her would-be attacker and, with remarkable calmness said, 'I am a Christian. The Lord Jesus Christ is watching over me right now, and He is not going to allow anything to happen to me He doesn't want to occur.'

Well at this, the man just stared at her with a blank look, completely dumbfounded. So the woman continued, 'Jesus Christ loves you. He wants to come into your life and become your Lord and Savior.'

Then she asked rather pointedly, 'Have you ever had the gospel explained to you in a way you could understand it?'

The man lowered his knife and simply replied, 'No.'
The woman said, 'Well then, please, sit down.' For the next hour and a half, this young Christian woman discussed the claims of Christ with her would-be attacker. When she did, she soon learned that he was new in the area and had no friends, no money, no purpose or hope in life.

And so against all hope, this hopeful Christian in a seemingly hopeless situation, led this hopeless man to the Lord of Hope, Jesus Christ."[4]

Now folks, I'd say if ever there was a seeming hopeless situation, it had to be that one, right? But it didn't turn out that way, right? Why? Because people, we serve a God Who's bigger than any situation. No matter how bad things might be, He's promised to use it all for our maturity!

People of God, when are we going to learn that there are no hopeless situations. There are only Christians who have given up hope! I'm telling you, the longer we live like this, we're not only ceasing to be a Body of Hope, but we're actually turning into a **Body of Despair**.

Oh, but that's not all. The **second reason** we look so hopeless is because we've forgotten we've been given a **Super Afterlife**.

1 Corinthians 15:16-17,19 "If there is no resurrection of the dead, then Christ has not been raised. And if Christ has not been raised, then your faith is useless, and you are still under condemnation for your sins. And if we have hope in Christ only for this life, we are the most miserable people in the world."

Now folks, according to our text, the Bible is clear. God not only gives us stability in the midst of a painful life, but He what? He gives us the promise of a super afterlife, right? Therefore, since our hope is in heaven and not in this life only, we what? We don't have to live miserable lives like everyone else in the world, right? Isn't that great news!

People, the point is this. Surely the American Church knows this, right? I mean, surely we know better than to get tricked into living a miserable life by only living for this world, right? People, Are you kidding? I mean, you've been there. You go into the average Church service today and what do you see? You don't see Christians praising God that they're going to heaven for all eternity. No! You see, them offering up prayer requests for the Dow Jones report and a good economy!

You might be thinking, "Well hey, I think you're being a little too unrealistic here. I mean, it's obvious you don't understand my concerns! If you saw how much time and work it takes to keep what little I have, you'd understand why I look so hopeless half the time!" Excuse me? People, what did our text say? If our only hope is to store up treasures in this life then we're guaranteed what? A miserable life. Why? Because nothing on earth is guaranteed to last! Only heaven is! Therefore, isn't it obvious if we place all our concerns in a place destined to perish, then sooner or later our hope will perish too? In fact, it's so obvious even these non-Christians figured it out:

"Recently, a man who had spent many summers in Maine, was fascinated by his companions who told about their experiences in a little town named Flagstaff. The town was to be flooded, as part of a large lake for which a dam was being built.

Because of this, in the months before it was to be flooded, all improvements and repairs in the whole town were stopped.

I mean, what was the use of painting a house if it were to be covered with water in six months? Why repair anything when the whole town was to be wiped out?

So week after week, the whole town became more and more focused on their new location and began to invest their lives in that. Why? Because they clearly understood it was a complete waste of time and money to secure their lives in that which was soon to be destroyed."[5]

Now folks, I'd say those people made the right decision, how about you? I mean, can you imagine how miserable they would've been if they kept pouring all their time and money in their old homes? Then people why is it a shocker that so many Christians are likewise miserable when all they do is hope for a powerful economy instead of a place in eternity?

People, when are we going to learn that there is no such thing as a hopeless life. There are only Christians who have given up hope in their afterlife! I'm telling you, the longer we live like this, we're not only ceasing to be a Body of Hope, but we're actually turning into a **Body of Dopes**.

Oh, but that's not all. The **third reason** we look so hopeless is because we've forgotten we've been given **Second Chances in Life**.

Hebrews 6:19-20 "We have this hope as an anchor for the soul, firm and secure. It enters the inner sanctuary behind the curtain, where Jesus, who went before us, has entered on our behalf. He has become a high priest forever, in the order of Melchizedek."

Now folks, according to our text, the Bible is clear. One of the most incredible things about the ministry of Jesus was not that He went to the cross to forgive us of most of our sin, but what? He became our forever High Priest to forgive us of all our sins, right? Therefore, because of His complete forgiveness, we're what? We're always guaranteed second chances in life, right? Man! Talk about a great hope, right?

The point is this. Surely the American Church knows this, right? I mean, surely we all know that no matter who we are or what we've done, we should never shun each other because Jesus will never shun us, right? People, Are you kidding? I mean, you've been there. You go into the average Church service today and what do you see? You don't see the Family of God accepting each other no matter what they've done. No! You see, them gossiping and shunning each other till kingdom come!

You might be thinking, "Well hey, I think you're being a little too liberal here. I mean, it's obvious you don't know this person like I do. I mean, if only you knew their background and know what I know, you know?" Excuse me? I could personally give a rip what you know. In fact, it's obvious the one thing you don't know is what it means to be a Christian. People, one of the greatest God-given hopes is not only in being given a stable life or even a super afterlife. It's this. It's in being given an endless supply of second chances in this life!

People, no wonder the Bible calls this an anchor for the soul. I mean, stop and think about it. What better hope is there in an unloving, unforgiving world to know that at least in the Church of Jesus Christ, you will never be shunned, you will never be rejected, you will always be accepted no matter who you are or what you've done, right? Unfortunately, not everyone seems to have figured this out yet. I'm going to share a story from a former Pastor about how a particular Church treated a girl in need of hope and I want you to tell me how well they did:

"I was a Pastor of a Church when I was a young man. And I remember going to visit a young woman who was pregnant out of wedlock. When I got to her house, there was the awareness that the Holy Spirit was with me. When I stepped into that living room, the Spirit of God was working in that woman and when I laid out the plan of salvation to her she responded and gave her life to Christ.

The next Sunday she came to Church services. And she came the Sunday after that and after that and after that, for a month and a half, but then she stopped coming.

So when I went to see her I said, 'What's wrong?'

She said, 'I can't come to your Church services anymore.'

And I said, 'Why?'

She said, 'Because I feel guilty and dirty and filthy in your congregation.'

I said, 'Jesus has forgiven you. Jesus has forgotten and blotted out your sin.'

I'll never forget her saying to me, 'Jesus may have forgiven. And Jesus may have forgotten. But the people in the congregation...they haven't forgiven. And they haven't forgotten.'

Please, on the subjective level, we in the Church have the capacity to make people feel guilty long after Jesus has forgiven them.'"

Now folks, I'd say that Church wasn't doing a very good job of being a Body of Hope, how about you? In fact, I'd say they looked more like a Body of Hypocrites, how about you? The point is this. It not only affected their walk with Christ, but what did it do? It kept that girl from walking in hope with Christ!

People, if we can't stop playing Church instead of being the Church then maybe it's time to get out of the Church! Why? Because being a Christian is not a game. What we say and do literally affects the eternal destiny of people around us. Therefore, it's high time we get rid of our practical amnesia. We have to remember who we are! We're not a bunch of hopeless hypocrites. Are you kidding? We are the Church of Jesus Christ. We are a **Body of Hope!**

Chapter Five

A Body of Joy

"One day two guys were talking at work and one of them began telling the other about all the problems he was having in his family.

After awhile the other guy said, 'Oh yeah? You think you got family problems? Well, that's nothing! Listen to this.

A few years ago I met a young widow with a grown-up daughter and we got married. After that, my father married my stepdaughter. So that made my stepdaughter my stepmother and my father became my stepson, and my wife became mother-in-law of her father-in-law.

But, that's not all! One day, the daughter of my wife, who is now my stepmother, had a son. Well, this made him my half-brother because he was my father's son. But, it also made him the son of my wife's daughter and at the same time my wife's grandson, which now made me grandfather of my own half-brother.

Oh, but that's still not all! One day my wife and I had a son, which made the sister of my son his grandmother and at the same time my mother-in-law. Not only that, it also made my father the brother-in-law of my own child whose stepsister is now my father's wife.

Because of this, I became my stepmother's brother-in-law. My wife is her own child's aunt. My son is my father's nephew and now I'm my own grandpa!'"[1]

Now folks, depending what part of the country you come from, I know some of you may be thinking, "Hey Preacher! You've gone too far this time. That ain't funny at all!" Besides that, I bet you're also thinking that family was just a little bit mixed up, you know what I'm saying? Folks, believe it or not, do you know there's a family even more mixed up than that one? Can anybody guess who that family is? Hey, that's right! It's the Family of God when we act like we have practical amnesia! Talk about being mixed up!

Oh, we say we know who we are as the Church, but half the time, with our lips and with our lives, we act like we've forgotten who we are. It's not only detrimental in our walk with Christ. It keeps others from believing in Christ. Therefore, to avoid this atrocity of Christians living like they have practical amnesia by not knowing who they are, we're going to continue our study from the Word of God on the people of God entitled, "**The Character of the Church.**"

We've already seen the first thing we need to know about the Church if we're going to stop acting like we have practical amnesia is that the Church is the Body of Christ. The second thing is that the Church is a Body of Brides. The third thing is that the Church is a Body of One. In the last chapter we saw the fourth thing we need to know is that the Church is a Body of Hope. There we saw, believe it or not, how the American Church is actually looking hopeless when the Bible says we should be hopeful. Why? Because we've forgotten that we've been given a stable life, a super afterlife, and an endless supply of second chances in life. Because of that, we're not only ceasing to be a Body of Hope, we're actually turning into a Body of despair and dopes. I don't think that's the kind of Church Jesus came to die for, how about you?

People, believe it or not, do you know that's not the only thing we need to know about the Church if we're going to stop acting like we have practical amnesia? The **fifth thing** we need to know is **The Church is a Body of Joy**. But hey, don't take my word for it. Let's listen to God's:

John 15:9-11 "As the Father has loved me, so have I loved you. Now remain in my love. If you obey my commands, you will remain in my love, just as I have obeyed my Father's commands and remain in his love. I have told you this so that my joy may be in you and that your joy may be complete."

Now folks, according to our text, the Bible is clear. When you and me are obedient in our walk with God, we're not only filled with the love of God, we're filled with what? We're filled with the joy of God, right? Notice is wasn't just a little joy. It's so much joy that we're completely filled with it for all the world to see, right?

Here's my point. Surely, we all know that, right? I mean, surely every Christian who has ever lived knows that the Church is to be a Body of Joy, where people look at us and say, "Wow! Now there's a group of people who never get depressed and are always full of smiles," right? Well, you'd think so, but we've have some problems. Why? Because if you look at most Churches it doesn't look like we're shouting for joy for all the world to see. Are you kidding? It looks like we're singing "gloom, despair, and agony on thee!"

So, why in the world would Christians look so joyless when the Bible says we should be so joyful? Hey, great question. I'm glad you asked. It's pretty simple. The **first reason** we look so joyless is because we've **Lost the Joy of Our Salvation**.

Habakkuk 3:17-18 "Even though the fig trees have no blossoms, and there are no grapes on the vine; even though the olive crop fails, and the fields lie empty and barren; even though the flocks die in the fields, and the cattle barns are empty, yet I will rejoice in the LORD! I will be joyful in the God of my salvation."

Now folks, according to our text, the Bible is clear. Even if our whole world is falling apart and crumbling all around us, we can still what? We can still rejoice in God. Why? Because our joy's not based on what happens to us externally. It's based on what happens to us eternally, right? It's based upon our salvation in God.

People, the point is this. Surely the American Church knows this, right? I mean, surely we'd never lose the joy of being saved, right? I mean, surely being saved from eternal destruction in hell is enough to keep us smiling for the rest of our lives, right? People, are you kidding? I mean, you've been there. You go into the average Church service today and what do you see? You don't see Christians excited about their future place in heaven. Are you kidding? It looks like they're already planted six feet under! Don't believe me? Just ask Oliver Wendell Holmes. He said this: "Hey, I might have entered the ministry if so many Christians didn't look and act like they were undertakers."[2]

You might be thinking, "Okay, so I'm not the most positive person in the world. Maybe I've gotten a little down in the dumps over the years since I got saved. So what? What's the big deal?" Big deal? I'll tell you what the big deal is. What did we read in our text? It's the joy of God's salvation that keeps us positive no matter the negative, right? Therefore, if we lose that joy, guess what's going to happen? We'll become negative no matter the positive, right? People, the next thing you know, you're going to end up like this one guy:

"Jim Smith went to Church service on Sunday morning. He heard the organist miss a note during the prelude and he winced. He saw a teenager talking when everybody was supposed to be bowed in silent prayer. He felt like the usher was watching to see what he put in the offering plate and it made him boil.

He caught the preacher making a slip of the tongue five times in the sermon by actual count. As he slipped out through the side door during the closing hymn, he muttered to himself, 'Never again, what a bunch of clods and hypocrites!'

Ron Jones went to Church service one Sunday morning. He heard the organist play an arrangement of 'A Mighty Fortress' and he was thrilled at the majesty of it. He heard a young girl take a moment in the service to speak a simple message of how her faith had made a difference in her life.

He was glad to see that the Church was sharing in a special offering for the hungry children of Nigeria. He especially appreciated the sermon that Sunday—it answered a question that had bothered him for a long time.

He thought as he walked out the doors, 'How can a man come here and not feel the presence of God?'

Both men went to the same Church service, on the same Sunday morning. And each one found what he was looking for."[3]

Now folks, I know this might be a rough question, but how many of you would say that first guy probably lost the joy of his salvation? Because of that he got just a little bit negative, right? Uh huh, slightly! People, the point is this. A life of negativity will not only ruin your reality, but it'll give a rotten impression of Christianity! Why? Because when we live like that, we're not just ceasing to be a Body of Joy. We're acting like a **Body of Depression**. If that's all I ever saw from Christians, I'd never want to be one, how about you?

Oh, but that's not all. The **second reason** we look so joyless is because we've **Lost Our Trust in God's Provision**.

1 Thessalonians 5:16-18 "Be joyful always; pray continually; give thanks in all circumstances, for this is God's will for you in Christ Jesus."

Now folks, according to our text, the Bible is clear. We can not only be full of joy once in a while but what? We can be full of joy all the while. How? By not only giving up prayers to God, but what? In giving up thanks to God, right? Why? Because our joy's not based on external circumstances. It's based on God Who's in control of our circumstances, right?

People, the point is this. Surely the American Church knows this, right? I mean, surely we know that God is faithful to give us not necessarily what we want but certainly what we need and so we're always joyful and thankful no matter what, right? People, Are you kidding? I mean, you've been there. You go into the average Church service today and what do you see? You don't see Christians full of excitement over the way God orders their life. Are you kidding? It looks like they've been sucking the end off of an exhaust pipe! Don't believe me? Just ask Billy Sunday. He said this" "To see some Christians you'd think an essential to being one is to have a face so long you could eat oatmeal out of the end of a gas pipe."[4]

You might be thinking, "Okay, so I'm not the most thankful person in the world. Maybe I've gotten a little bit ungrateful over the years since I got saved, so what? What's the big deal?" Big deal? I'll tell you what the big deal is. What did our text say? It's a trust in God's provision that keeps us what? It keeps us joyful and thankful no matter the circumstance, right? Therefore, if we lose that trust, guess what's going to happen? We'll become thankless even though we should be thankful, right? Once we do that, our joy goes right out the window! And to show you how easy it is for us to slip into this unhealthy mode of thinking, we're going to take a little test. Let's see if we can remember just how to be thankful:

- If you find yourself stuck in traffic, don't get upset. Think of the people in the world where driving is an unheard privilege.

- If you have a bad day at work, then think of the person who's been out of work for years.

- If you despair over a relationship gone bad, then think of the person who has never known what it's like to be loved in return.

- If you grieve the passing of another weekend, then think of the woman in dire straits, working twelve hours a day, seven days a week to feed her children.

- If your car should break down, leaving you miles away from assistance, then think of the paraplegic who would love the opportunity to take that walk.

- If you should notice a new gray hair in the mirror, then think of the cancer patient in chemotherapy who wishes they had hair to examine at all.

- If you find yourself the victim of other people's bitterness, ignorance, smallness or insecurities, then think about it. Things could be worse. You could be one of them.[5]

Now folks, I'd say if you stop to think about it, there really is no reason to be ungrateful and lose our joy is there? In fact, I'd say God's doing a pretty good job providing for us after all, right? People, the point is this. A life of ungratefulness will not only ruin your reality, but it'll give a rotten impression of Christianity! Why? Because when we live like that, we're not just ceasing to be a Body of Joy. We're acting like a **Body of Whiners**. If that's all I ever saw from Christians, I'd never want to be one, how about you?

Oh, but that's not all. The **third reason** we look so joyless is because we've **Lost Our Sense of Celebration**.

Acts 2:44,46-47 "And all the believers met together constantly and shared everything they had. They worshiped together at the Temple each day, met in homes for the Lord's Supper, and shared their meals with great joy and generosity. Everyone liked them, and each day the Lord added to their group others who were being saved."

Now folks, according to our text, the Bible is clear. The early Church not only shared good food with each other, but they shared what? They shared great joy with each other, right? Because of this what happened? Every single day God was saving tons of people, right? Why? Because stop and think about it people! Who in the world wouldn't want to be a Christian if you not only saw them full of joy here and there, but you saw them full of joy everywhere, right?

The point is this. Surely the American Church knows this, right? I mean, surely we know that when we gather together it's a time to celebrate and sing for joy, right? People, Are you kidding? I mean, you've been there. You go into the average Church service today and what do you see? You don't see the Family of God celebrating His salvation and control in their lives. Are you kidding? You see them cold and stiff as if they had no life!

You might be thinking, "Okay, so I'm not the most enthusiastic person in the world when I go to Church services. Maybe I've lost a little bit of that excitement I had when I first got saved, so what? What's the big deal?" Big deal? I'll tell you what the big deal is. Have you ever been in a Church service that's devoid of joy? It doesn't look like a praise service. It looks like a funeral service! Therefore, in order to make sure that doesn't happen to us, I'm going to share a story about a Christian and his day in the world and you tell me if he still have his sense of celebration in life:

"I got on an elevator in a high rise apartment in New York City and it was filled with dead people! Did you ever get on an elevator with dead people who are just standing there dead?

As the elevator doors closed I said to myself, 'Who are these dead people? Maybe I'm dead. If we're dead, where are we going?' I was relieved when the elevator went up!

When the door closed, I did what you're not supposed to do. I turned and faced the crowd. Now, people are used to getting on elevators and turning to face the door and looking up to stare at the numbers. So the next time you get on an elevator, get on, turn around and face everyone and smile. It blows them away. They do not know how to handle this.

And I said to these people, 'Lighten up! It's a seventy-fifth floor express and we're going to be traveling together for a while.'

And these sophisticated New Yorkers started to back up away from me so I said, 'What do you say...we sing!' And these suckers were so intimidated by me...they did! I mean you should have been there. They started singing, 'You are my sunshine, my only sunshine.'

I got off at the seventieth floor and this guy got off with me and I asked, 'Are you going to the same meeting I'm going to?' And he said, 'No...I just wanted to finish the song!'

Please people. Please understand. The world is dead and I consider it my God-given responsibility to resurrect the dead wherever I go!"

Now folks, I know this might be a tough question, but how many of you guys would say that Christian still has his sense of celebration in life? By the way, how many of you guys are going to try that the next time you get on an elevator? Uh huh, sure. People, stop and think about it. Isn't that the way we should walk around in life? I mean, shouldn't we be full of so much joy that God uses us to raise the dead wherever we go? Why? Because we have reasons to celebrate! We're not going to hell. We're going to heaven. God's not only in control of our afterlife, He's in control of this life! Therefore, we should be celebrating twenty-four hours a day, right?

People, let's be honest. How many Christians do you know like that? Or worse yet, how many Church services have you been to that celebrate like that? If you still don't think losing your sense of celebration is a big deal, then maybe you should hear what Phillip Brooks said: "The religion that makes a man look sick certainly won't cure the world."[6] Why? Because stop and think about it! Who in the world would ever want to be a Christian if all they ever saw were Church services full of dead people?

People, if we can't stop playing Church instead of being the Church then maybe it's time to get out of the Church. Why? Because being a Christian is not a game. What we say and do literally affects the eternal destiny of people around us. Therefore, it's high time we get rid of our practical amnesia. We have to remember who we are! We're not a bunch of lifeless dead people. Are you kidding? We are the Church of Jesus Christ. We are a **Body of Joy**!

Chapter Six

A Body of Love

Hey, how many of you guys remember that lady named Stella who sued McDonald's and won 2.9 million dollars because she spilled hot coffee in her own lap? Remember that lady? Ever since then, they've come out with what's called the Stella Award for outrageous behavior like hers. How many of you have heard of those? Well, for those of you who may have forgotten, I'm here to help you out. I'm going to share with you some of the winners of the Stella Awards and you tell me if their behavior is just a little bit outrageous.

- In January 2000, Kathleen Robertson of Austin, Texas was awarded by a jury $780,000 after breaking her ankle inside of a furniture store after tripping over a toddler who was running around in the store. The owners of the store were understandably surprised at the verdict, considering the fact that the misbehaving toddler was Mrs. Robertson's own son.

- In June 1998, 19 year-old Carl Truman of Los Angeles won $74,000 and medical expenses when his neighbor ran over his hand with a Honda Accord. And apparently the problem was that Carl didn't notice his neighbor was behind the wheel of the car when he was trying to steal the hubcaps off his neighbor's car.

- In October 1998, Terrence Dickson of Bristol, Pennsylvania was leaving a house he had just robbed by way of the garage. However, he was unable to get the garage door open since the automatic door opener was malfunctioning. And neither could he re-enter the house because the door connecting the house to the garage locked when he pulled it shut. And since the family of the house he robbed was on vacation, Mr. Dickson found himself locked in the garage for eight days where he was able to stay alive on a case of Pepsi he found and a bag of dog food. So that's right, he sued the homeowner's insurance, claiming the situation caused him undue mental anguish. And believe it or not, the jury agreed to the tune of half a million dollars.

- But the all time winner is Mr. Merv Grazinski of Oklahoma City. In November 2000, Mr. Grazinski purchased a brand new 32-foot Winnebago motor home. And on his first trip home, having just entered the freeway, he set the cruise control at 70 mph and calmly left the drivers seat to go into the back and make himself a cup of coffee. Not surprisingly, the motor home left the freeway, crashed and overturned. That's right, Mr. Grazinski sued Winnebago for not advising him in the handbook that he shouldn't do this and he was awarded $1,750,000 plus a new Winnebago. And believe it or not, Winnebago actually changed their handbooks after this court case just in case other Grazinski's are still at large out there![1]

Now folks, I'd say that's some pretty outrageous behavior, how about you? Uh huh, slightly! But folks, believe it or not, do you know there's some even more outrageous behavior than that? And get this. It's not being done by a handful of people once a year, but it's being done by millions of people everyday of the year! Can anybody guess who this is? Hey, that's right! It's the American Church when we act like we have practical amnesia! Talk about outrageous behavior!

Oh, we say we know who we are as the Church, but half the time, with our lips and with our lives, we act like we've forgotten who we are. It's not only detrimental in our walk with Christ. It keeps others from believing in Christ. Therefore, to avoid this atrocity of Christians living like they have practical amnesia by not knowing who they are, we're going to continue our study from the Word of God on the people of God entitled, "**The Character of the Church**."

We've already seen the first thing we need to know about the Church if we're going to stop acting like we have practical amnesia is that the Church is the Body of Christ. The second thing is that the Church is a Body of Brides. The third thing is that the Church is a Body of One. The fourth thing is that the Church is a Body of Hope. In the last chapter we saw the fifth thing we need to know is that the Church is a Body of Joy. There we saw, believe it or not, how the American Church is actually behaving joyless when the Bible says we should be joyful. Why? Because we've lost the joy of our salvation, a trust in God's provision, and our sense of celebration. Because of that, we're not only ceasing to be a Body of Joy, we're actually turning into a Body of depressing dead people. I don't think that's the kind of Church Jesus came to die for, how about you?

People, believe it or not, do you know that's not the only thing we need to know about the Church if we're going to stop acting like we have practical amnesia? The **sixth thing** we need to know is **The Church is a Body of Love**. But hey, don't take my word for it. Let's listen to God's:

John 13:33-35 "My children, I will be with you only a little longer. You will look for me, and just as I told the Jews, so I tell you now: Where I am going, you cannot come. A new command I give you: Love one another. As I have loved you, so you must love one another. By this all men will know that you are my disciples, if you love one another."

Now folks, according to our text, the Bible is clear. If you and me want the world to know we really belong to Jesus, what do we have to do? We have to love one another right? Why? Because if people who have never seen Jesus are going to believe in Jesus, then the followers of Jesus must love like Jesus, right?

Here's my point. Surely, we all know that, right? I mean, surely every Christian who has ever lived knows that the Church is to be a Body of Love, where people look at us and say, "Wow! Now there's a group of people who always gets along and goes out of their way to help others. They must be disciples of Christ," right? Well, you'd think so, but we have some problems. Why? Because if you look at most Churches it doesn't look like we're full of the love of God for all the world to see. Are you kidding? It looks like we're full of hatred, strife, and animosity!

So, why in the world would Christians look so loveless when the Bible says we should be so loving? Hey, great question. I'm glad you asked. It's pretty simple. The **first reason** we look so loveless is because **We Refuse to Love the Needy**.

James 1:27 "Religion that God our Father accepts as pure and faultless is this: to look after orphans and widows in their distress and to keep oneself from being polluted by the world."

Now folks, according to our text, the Bible is clear. If we want our relationship with God to be considered pure and faultless, what do we have to do? We not only have to stay away from the pollution of this world, but what? We have to give away God's love to the people of the world, right? Notice to whom this love is directed towards. It's to the who? To the widows and orphans, to those who are needy, right?

People, the point is this. Surely the American Church knows this, right? I mean, surely we know that we're to love the needy if we're going to keep a tight relationship with God because after all, that's what Jesus did when He was on earth, right? People, are you kidding? I mean, you've been there. You go into the average Church service today and what do you see? You don't see Christians busting their backs taking care of the needy. No! You see them folding their arms being selfish and greedy!

You might be thinking, "Okay, so I don't go out of my way to personally get involved with the needs of others. You don't understand. I just don't have the time. I mean, I'm just trying to take care of my own needs let alone someone else's. Besides, those people kind of creep me out and don't we have government programs for them?" Excuse me? Have you not read your Bible? What did Jesus do? He wasn't just concerned about His needs. Are you kidding? And He certainly didn't cast off His responsibility to help others on to a government program. No people! Read your Bible! He went out of His way and sacrificed his time day in and day out again and again to hang out with the who? The tax collectors, the sinners, the prostitutes; the outcasts of society, right?

Therefore, if that's what Jesus did when He was on earth, then what do you think His followers who are still on earth should be doing? The very same thing, right? Why? Because people when we die and stand before God, He's not going to ask us how much stuff we had in life. Are you kidding? He's going to ask us how much of His love you gave away in life, just like Jesus did! That's right, for those weird people down south who may have forgotten this, we're going to take a little test. Let's see what God's going to ask us on the other side so we can see how well we're doing on this side:

- Do you know that God won't ask what kind of car you drove? He'll ask how many people you drove who didn't have a car.

- Do you know that God won't ask in what neighborhood you lived? He'll ask how you treated your neighbors.

- Do you know that God won't ask the square footage of your house? He'll ask how many people you welcomed into your house.

- Do you know that God won't ask about the clothes you had in your closet? He'll ask how many people you gave clothes to.

- Do you know that God won't ask what your highest salary was? He'll ask if you used your salary to be a blessing to others.

- Do you know that God won't ask what your job title was? He'll ask if you shared His love with the people at your job.

- Do you know that God won't ask how many friends you had? He'll ask how many people you were a friend to.

- Do you know that God won't ask about what kind of physical shape you were in? He'll ask how well you took care of the physical needs of others.[2]

Now folks, I'd say there's going to be a whole lot of Christians failing that test when they meet God one day, how about you? Uh huh, slightly!

People, the point is this. If you want to live like that as a Christian and fail the test in the end, I guess that's you're prerogative. I feel sorry for you. But what you need to know is it doesn't stop there! When you and me as Christians refuse to love the needy, we're not just jeopardizing our walk with Christ. We're keeping other people from believing in Christ! Why? Because when all we do is live for our needs, ourselves, our stuff, what in the world are we doing? We're not just ceasing to be a Body of Love. We're acting like a **Body of Greed**. If that's all I ever saw from people who were supposed to be followers of Christ, I'd never want to follow Christ, how about you?

Oh, but that's not all. The **second reason** we look so loveless is because **We Refuse to Love Our Enemies**.

Romans 12:19,20 "Dear friends, never avenge yourselves. Leave that to God. Instead, do what the Scriptures say. If your enemies are hungry, feed them. If they are thirsty, give them something to drink, and they will be ashamed of what they have done to you."

Now folks, according to our text, the Bible is clear. The best way to get rid of your enemies is to what? Treat them like your friends, right?

We don't get revenge on them for what they do? No! We take them out to lunch for a cheeseburger or two!

People, the point is this. Surely the American Church knows this, right? I mean, surely we know that we're to love our enemies if they're going to become our friends because after all, that's what Jesus did when He was on earth, right? People, are you kidding? I mean, you've been there. You go into the average Church service today and what do you see? You don't see Christians loving their enemies and seeking a truce. Are you kidding? You see them fighting an eye for an eye and a tooth for a tooth!

You might be thinking, "Okay, so I don't make it a point to treat my enemies like friends. But you don't understand. You don't know what they did to me and how wrong it was. Besides, they don't deserve to be treated like a friend." Excuse me? Have you not read your Bible? What did Jesus do? He didn't just love those who loved Him. Are you kidding? He voluntarily died on the cross for who? For his enemies, for people like you and me who hated his guts, right? I'd say we don't deserve to be loved like that, right?

Therefore, if that's what Jesus did when He was on earth, then what do you think His followers who are still on earth should be doing? The very same thing, right? Why? Because people when we love our enemies just like Jesus did it turns out to be one of the most profound ways to share the gospel. In fact, it might be the only way to reach some people for the Lord. That's right. For those of you who may not know of what loving your enemies looks like in real life, I'm going to share with you a true story of a man named Rhett. You tell me if his love for his enemy didn't have a profound affect on him:

"It was a seemingly normal day at work for this average American Christian named Rhett Falkner. Only little did he know that on this day, an enemy was going to start working right beside him. So being a Christian and all, Rhett felt he should go out of his way to welcome this new employee and so he said hello and introduced himself.

That's when the trouble started. As soon as this enemy found out Rhett was a Christian he began to laugh and make fun of him and declare how stupid Christians were. So what did Rhett do? He promptly invited his enemy over for supper to give him a chance to meet his family.

Even a nice home-cooked meal with a pleasant family didn't seem to make a dent with this enemy. He merely continued his tirade about how Christians were a bunch of mindless brainwashed idiots who had to have somebody else tell them how to think. So what did Rhett do? He invited his friend to a Christian singles group because he knew his enemy would never go to a regular Sunday Church service.

While he was there, his enemy defied the leader during the devotion time by staring at him in anger the whole time and even refused to bow his head in prayer. When it was time to ask for prayer requests and others were praying for their loved ones to be saved or healed, this enemy spoke up in complete mockery of God and asked everyone to pray for the dying slugs and snails in the world. So what did Rhett do? He simply prayed to God on behalf of the dying slugs in the world, just like his enemy requested.

One day Rhett told his enemy that his family was moving back to New York and he'd probably never see him again. But even despite the fact that Rhett had continually invited his enemy into his own home, constantly took him out to eat for free, chauffeured him around town with his own gas, his enemy didn't even say goodbye. So what did Rhett do? He simply kept praying for his enemy even though they were miles apart.

That's when months later, at another workplace 3,000 miles away, Rhett got a call from his old enemy. Naturally, being surprised by the call, Rhett asked his enemy why he was calling him. As it turned out, Rhett's former enemy had not only become his friend, but he was now his brother in the Lord. Why? All because Rhett's love for his enemy had enabled him become a Christian as well. "[3]

Now folks, I'd say Rhett's love for his enemy had a profound effect on his enemy, how about you? By the way, in case you haven't guessed, Rhett's enemy was me!

People, the point is this. When are we going to realize that when you and me as Christians refuse to love our enemies, we're not just jeopardizing our walk with Christ, we're actually keeping others from believing in Christ! Trust me! I was one of them! People, that's why we have to wake up and realize when all we do is repay others with an eye for an eye and a tooth for a tooth, what in the world do you think we're doing? We're not just ceasing to be a Body of Love. We're acting like a **Body of Vengeance**. If that's all I ever saw from people who were supposed to be followers of Christ, I'd never want to follow Christ, how about you?

Oh, but that's not all. The **third reason** we look so loveless is because **We Refuse to Love God's Family**.

1 John 3:10 "This is how we know who the children of God are and who the children of the devil are. Anyone who does not do what is right is not a child of God; nor is anyone who does not love his brother."

Now folks, according to our text, the Bible is clear. If you and me want to prove that we're no longer a child of the devil but now have become a child of God, what do we have to do? We have to love the family of God, right?

The point is this. Surely the American Church knows this, right? I mean, surely we know that we need to love not just the needy or even our enemies, but we have to love God's family, right? I mean, of all three of those, surely that's the easiest one, right? People, are you kidding? I mean, you've been there. You go into the average Church service today and what do you see? You don't see Christians loving each other because God loves them. Are you kidding? You see them kicking, screaming and causing tons of division!

You might be thinking, "Okay, so I don't get along with everyone in the Church. But you see, you don't understand. You have no idea what they said to me and how wrong it was. Because of that, they don't deserve to be my friend!" Excuse me? People, what did the text say? When you and me act like this we're acting like what? Not like a child of God but who? A child of the devil! If you want to live like that as a Christian, I guess that's your prerogative. I feel sorry for you. What you need to know is it doesn't stop there! Why? Because a hypocritical lack of love for God's family will not only kill a Church, it will kill people's desire to be a part of the Church, like it did with this man:

"Years ago in Germany there was a young Jewish boy who had a profound sense of admiration for his father. The life of the family centered around the acts of piety and devotion prescribed by their religion. The father was zealous in attending worship and instruction and demanded the same from his children.

When the boy was a teenager the family was forced to move to another town in Germany. In the new location there was no synagogue, and the pillars of the community all belonged to the Lutheran Church. Suddenly, the father announced to the family that they were all going to abandon their Jewish traditions and join the Lutheran Church.

When the stunned family asked why, the father explained that it was necessary to help his business. Of course, the young boy was bewildered and confused. Pretty soon his deep disappointment gave way to anger and bitterness that plagued him throughout his life. One day when he was old enough, he left Germany and went to England to study.

He sat daily at the British Museum formulating his ideas and composing a book. In that book he introduced a whole new way of life and a worldview that was designed to change the world. And also in that book he described religion as an 'opiate for the masses.'

Today there are billions of people in the world who live under the system invented by this embittered man. His name is Karl Marx. The influence of this father's hypocrisy is still being felt around the world."[4]

Now folks, I'd say one man's hypocrisy had a profound effect on his son, how about you? People, the point is this. If that one man's hypocrisy birthed communism, which by the way has killed millions of people, can you imagine how many more millions of people have died and gone to hell over the Church's hypocrisy? What hypocrisy? Well, what do you think we're doing when we don't love each other as God's family? We're not just ceasing to be a Body of Love, we're acting like a hypocritical **Body of Hate**. No wonder people don't want to become Christians!

People, if we can't stop playing Church instead of being the Church then maybe it's time to get out of the Church. Why? Because being a Christian is not a game. What we say and do literally affects the eternal destiny of people around us. Therefore, it's high time we get rid of our practical amnesia. We have to remember who we are! We're not a bunch of greedy, vengeful, hate-filled people. Are you kidding? We are the Church of Jesus Christ. We are a **Body of Love**!

Chapter Seven

A Body of Peace

I know this might come as a surprise to some of you, but how many of you guys have learned this lesson in life? The longer you live, the older you get. Have you learned that one? It's a shocker, isn't it? The only thing wrong with getting older is just when you finally get your head together your body starts falling apart! Have you noticed that? Well, for you young whippersnappers out there who think it could never happen to you, that's right, I'm here to help you out. I came across a list of some surefire signs you're getting older, or should I say more mature. Let's see take a look:

1. At the breakfast table you hear snap, crackle, pop and you're not eating cereal.

2. You and your teeth don't sleep together anymore.

3. You wake up looking like your driver's license picture.

4. You sit in a rocking chair and you can't get it going.

5. Everything hurts and what doesn't hurt doesn't work anymore.

6. The twinkle in your eye is merely a reflection of the sun on your bifocals.

7. You have more patience, but it's actually because you just don't care anymore.

8. You look for your glasses for half an hour before you realize they were on your head the whole time.

9. You sink your teeth into a steak and they stay there.

10. You try to straighten out the wrinkles in your socks and discover you aren't wearing any.[1]

Yes, the signs are quite obvious when you're getting more mature in life, aren't they? But folks, believe it or not, do you know the signs are just as obvious when you're getting more immature in life? I'm not talking just physically. I'm talking spiritually as well. Can anybody guess what those obvious signs of spiritual immaturity are? Hey, that's right! It's when we act like we have practical amnesia! Talk about immature behavior!

Oh, we say we know who we are as the Church, but half the time, with our lips and with our lives, we act like we've forgotten who we are. It's not only detrimental in our walk with Christ. It keeps others from believing in Christ. Therefore, to avoid this atrocity of Christians living like they have practical amnesia by not knowing who they are, we're going to continue our study from the Word of God on the people of God entitled, "**The Character of the Church**."

We've already seen the first thing we need to know about the Church if we're going to stop acting like we have practical amnesia is that the Church is the Body of Christ. The second thing is that the Church is a Body of Brides. The third thing is that the Church is a Body of One. The fourth thing is that the Church is a Body of Hope. The fifth thing is that the Church is a Body of Joy. In the last chapter we saw the sixth thing we need to know is that the Church is a Body of Love. There we saw, believe it or not, how the American Church is actually behaving loveless when the Bible says we should be loving. Why? Because we refuse to love the needy, we refuse to love our enemies, and we refuse to love God's family. Because of that, we're not only ceasing to be a Body of Love, we're actually turning into a Body of greedy, vengeful, hate-filled people. I don't think that's the kind of Church Jesus came to die for, how about you?

People, believe it or not, do you know that's not the only thing we need to know about the Church if we're going to stop acting like we have practical amnesia? The **seventh thing** we need to know is **The Church is a Body of Peace**. But hey, don't take my word for it. Let's listen to God's:

John 14:23-27 "Jesus replied, If anyone loves me, he will obey my teaching. My Father will love him, and we will come to him and make our home with him. He who does not love me will not obey my teaching. These words you hear are not my own; they belong to the Father who sent me. All this I have spoken while still with you. But the Counselor, the Holy Spirit, whom the Father will send in my name, will teach you all things and will remind you of everything I have said to you. Peace I leave with you; my peace I give you. I do not give to you as the world gives. Do not let your hearts be troubled and do not be afraid."

Now folks, according to our text, the Bible is clear. Jesus not only promised to send us His Spirit after He left, but He what? He promised to give is His peace before He left, right? Notice He didn't say He might give us His peace. Neither did He say if we grunt and groan He'd think about giving us some peace. No! What did He say? He said I give you my peace right now, right?

Here's my point. Surely, we all know that, right? I mean, surely every Christian who has ever lived knows that the Church is to be a Body of Peace, where people look at us and say, "Wow! Now there's a group of people who are always calm, cool, collected and they never seem to get frazzled no matter what happens to them," right? Well, you'd think so, but we have some problems. Why? Because if you look at most Churches it doesn't look like we're full of peace. Are you kidding? It looks like we're falling to pieces!

So, why in the world would Christians look so peaceless when the Bible says we should be so peaceful? Hey, great question. I'm glad you asked. It's pretty simple. The **first reason** we look so peaceless is because **We've Forgotten How to Be Confident in God**.

Philippians 4:6-7 "Do not be anxious about anything, but in everything, by prayer and petition, with thanksgiving, present your requests to God. And the peace of God, which transcends all understanding, will guard your hearts and your minds in Christ Jesus."

Now folks, according to our text, the Bible is clear. Talk about some good news! You and I have divine permission from God to what? To never ever be anxious about what? About anything, right? Why? Because we pray in confidence that God's going to provide for us and when we do that, what happens? We're filled with what the peace of God, right?

People, the point is this. Surely the American Church knows this, right? I mean, surely we know that the peace of God is maintained not in having perfect surroundings but in being confident that God is in control of our surroundings, right? People, are you kidding? Let's be honest! We don't present our requests to God and walk away in peace. No! We skip that part and go straight to anxiety, right? People, this is not only a slap in the face of God, but if we're honest with ourselves, we place our confidence in all kinds of things without even thinking about it. Tell me the following statement isn't true:

"We go to doctors whose names we can't pronounce and whose degrees we've never verified, who give us prescriptions we cannot read. Then without question, we take it to a pharmacist we've never seen who gives us containers of chemicals we've never heard of and we go home and take them with instructions we don't understand, all in faith!"[2]

Therefore, if we automatically have confidence in a doctor we don't even know, then how much more should we be confident in the One Who created the doctor from head to toe? People, stop and think about it! Isn't God worthy of our confidence? Don't you think He knows how to provide for us? I mean, He's just God after all! Because we don't immediately put our confidence in God, we not only miss out on the peace of God, but half the time we don't even acknowledge His provision until after the fact, like these ladies did:

"Corrie Ten Boom and her sister Betsy had just been transferred to the worst German prison camp they'd been to yet called Ravensbruck. They, along with hundreds of other women were stripped of their few belongings and forced into a very small barrack. The problem was, it was not only cold and overcrowded, but it was infested with fleas.

But by a miracle of God, they managed to smuggle in a bible and so Corrie and Betsy would read it as often as they could for encouragement. And one morning they read the passage in the Bible that said to give God thanks in all things. So Betsy told Corrie they needed to stop and thank the Lord for everything, including the fleas.

Well, being frustrated and flea bitten, Corrie refused to give God thanks for those fleas. But her sister persisted until finally Corrie gave in begrudgingly.

But the good news was that during the months they spent in that flea infested barrack, these sisters were able to hold regular Bible studies to encourage many of the other hurting women there. And this of course was a huge risk because if the guards had caught them, they would have either tortured or killed them.

For some strange reason, the guards never seemed to notice. That's when several months later, they finally learned the reason why. You see, the guards would not enter their barracks because of all the fleas. "[3]

Now folks, I'd say when all was said and done, those ladies were just a little bit grateful for those fleas, how about you? I'd say they were at peace after that, how about you? People, this is the great news! We don't have to wait for an attack of the Killer Fleas before we receive the peace of God. No! Right now, today, if you place your confidence back in God guess what's going to happen? You're going to experience the peace of God no matter what happens! Why? Because that's what God said!

People, the point is this. If you don't want to place your confidence in God and be filled with anxiety, I guess that's your prerogative. I feel sorry for you. But what you need to know is it doesn't stop there! When we as Christians live like that we're not just harming our walk with Christ. We're keeping other people from believing in Christ! Why? Because stop and think about it! We're not just ceasing to be a Body of Peace. We're acting like a **Body of Worry**. If that's all the better a Christian's God could do, I wouldn't want to worship that God, how about you?

Oh, but that's not all. The **2ⁿᵈ reason** we look so peaceless is because **We've Forgotten How to Be Content in God**.

Philippians 4:11-13 "I am not saying this because I am in need, for I have learned to be content whatever the circumstances. I know what it is to be in need, and I know what it is to have plenty. I have learned the secret of being content in any and every situation, whether well fed or hungry, whether living in plenty or in want. I can do everything through him who gives me strength."

Now folks, according to our text, the Bible is clear. Talk about some good news! You and I can be what? We can be content in any and every situation if life, right? Why? Because just like Paul learned, God not only gives us strength no matter what happens to us, but He certainly knows what's best for us, right? Therefore, we can be content, right?

People, the point is this. Surely the American Church knows this, right? I mean, surely we know that the peace of God is maintained not in getting all we want for us but in being content that God will give us what's best for us, right? People, are you kidding? Let's be honest! We're not satisfied with what God gives us in life. No! We whine and complain over every detail in life!

People, the point is this. Stop and think about it! Shouldn't we be content with what God brings into our lives? I mean, don't you think He knows what's best for us? I mean, after all, He's just God, you know? Therefore, to help us see that God really does know what's best for us, even down to the most trivial of things, I'm going to share with you the seemingly trivial events that happened to some of the survivors of 911. And you tell me if they weren't just a little bit grateful for what God provided on that day:

- One person was late that day because his son started kindergarten.

- Another fellow was alive because it was his turn to bring donuts.

- One woman was late because her alarm clock didn't go off in time.

- One person's car wouldn't start.

- One person was late because they were stuck on the New Jersey Turnpike due to an auto accident.

- One guy missed his bus.

- One lady spilled food on her clothes and had to take time to change.

- One person had to go back in the house to answer the telephone.
- One person had a child that dawdled and didn't get ready as soon as they should have.

- One person couldn't get a taxi.

- One man put on a new pair of shoes that morning, but since they were new, he developed a blister on his foot. So he had to stop at a drugstore to buy a Band-Aid. That's the only reason why he's alive today.[4]

Now folks, I'd say when all was said and done, those people were just a little bit grateful for those trivial things that morning, how about you? I'd say they were at peace after that, how about you? People, this is the great news! We don't have to wait for an attack from Muslim terrorists before we receive the peace of God. No! Right now, today, if you determine to be content in God guess what's going to happen? You're going to experience the peace of God no matter what happens! Why? Because that's what God said!

People, the point is this. If you don't want to be content in God and be wigged out all your life, I guess that's you're prerogative. I feel sorry for you. But what you need to know is it doesn't stop there! When we as Christians live like that we're not just harming our walk with Christ. We're keeping other people from believing in Christ! Why? Because stop and think about it! We're not just ceasing to be a Body of Peace. We're acting like a **Body of Stress**. If that's all the better a Christian's God could do, I wouldn't want to worship that God, how about you?

Oh, but that's not all. The **3rd reason** we look so peaceless is because **We've Forgotten How to Be Courageous in God**.

John 16:28,33 "I came from the Father and entered the world; now I am leaving the world and going back to the Father. I have told you these things, so that in me you may have peace. In this world you will have trouble. But take heart! I have overcome the world."

Now folks, according to our text, the Bible is clear. Talk about some good news! No matter what trouble we may face in the world, we can what? We can still have peace in this world, right? Why? Because Jesus is in control of this troublesome world, right? Therefore, He must also be in control of our troublesome lives, right? Of course! That's why

He said to take heart! That's why we can always be courageous no mater what, right?

People, the point is this. Surely the American Church knows this, right? I mean, surely we know that the peace of God is maintained not by having a trouble-free life but by being courageous over God's control of our troubles in life, right? People, are you kidding? Let's be honest! We're not strong and courageous through thick and thin. No! We get all freaked out and scared over the slightest whim!

Therefore, in order to help us see that God really is in control of our lives, even our troubles, I'm going to share with you some serious troubles people had and you tell me if God didn't know what He was doing:

"One day, Abraham Lincoln had a problem. He and his partner's store was going bankrupt and even though he really wanted to study law, he was too poor to even buy one of the books he needed called Blackstone's Commentary on English Law.

But just then, a strange-looking wagon came up the road and when it got to Lincoln the driver said, 'I'm trying to move my family out west, and I'm out of money. I've got a good barrel here that I could sell for fifty cents.'

Even though Lincoln didn't have the money to spare, he looked at the man's wife whose face was thin and emaciated, and he took his last fifty cents and said, 'I reckon I could use a good barrel.'

All day long the barrel sat on the porch of that store and his partner kept telling him how foolish he was. But later that evening, Lincoln saw something in the bottom of the barrel under a pile of papers and when he reached in to pull it out it, he discovered it was a book. And standing there petrified, he read the title. Blackstone's Commentary on English Law."[5]

Oh, but that's not all.

"One day, in 1875 Ira Sankey, the song leader for Dwight Moody was traveling on a steamboat when someone just happened to ask him to sing a hymn. So he picked one out and sang it and when he did, a man stepped out of the shadows and asked him if he served in the Union Army doing guard duty in 1862?

When Ira said yes the man continued. He said, 'So did I, but I was serving in the Confederate army. When I saw you standing at your post I raised my gun to kill you but at that instant you raised your eyes to heaven and began to sing the song you sang just now.

As you did, I began to think of my childhood and my God-fearing mother because that was the same song she sang to me. Because of that, I couldn't kill you.'"[6]

Oh, but that's still not all.

"One day during WWII, an American B-17 bomber was making a bomb raid over Germany when their gas tanks were hit by the German flack fire, but for some reason they managed to make it back home.

So the next day, the pilot, reflecting on the miracle of a twenty-millimeter shell piercing the fuel tank without exploding the plane, went to go get that shell as a souvenir of unbelievable luck.

But that's when the crew chief told him that not just one shell but eleven shells had been found in the gas tanks and not a single one of them exploded.

So they sent the shells to the armory to be defused, but that's when they discovered all eleven shells were missing their explosive charges. For some strange reason they were as clean as a whistle and completely empty, except for one of them.

Believe it or not, inside that one shell was a carefully rolled up piece of paper. And on it written a message in the Czechoslovakian language that said this, 'This is all we can do for you now.'"[7]

Now folks, I'd say when all was said and done, those people had no doubt whatsoever that God was in control of their troubles, how about you? I'd say they were at peace after that, how about you? People, this is the great news! We don't have to wait for an attack from German artillery before we receive the peace of God. No! Right now, today, if you determine to be courageous in God guess what's going to happen? You're going to experience the peace of God no matter what happens! Why? Because that's what God said!

People, the point is this. If you don't want to place your courage in God and be scared all your life, I guess that's you're prerogative. I feel sorry for you. But what you need to know is that it doesn't stop there! When you and I as Christians live like that we're not just harming our walk with Christ. We're keeping other people from believing in Christ! Why? Because stop and think about it! We're not just ceasing to be a Body of Peace. We're acting like a **Body of Fear**. If that's all the better a Christian's God could do, I wouldn't want to worship that God, how about you?

People, if we can't stop playing Church instead of being the Church then maybe it's time to get out of the Church. Why? Because being a Christian is not a game. What we say and do literally affects the eternal destiny of people around us. Therefore, it's high time we get rid of our practical amnesia. We have to remember who we are! We're not a bunch of worried, stressed-out fearful people. Are you kidding? We are the Church of Jesus Christ. We are a **Body of Peace**!

Chapter Eight

A Body of Strangers

Hey, how many of you guys heard the saying, "Crime does not pay"? We all know that one, right? Of course we do. Why? Because committing a crime is not only unbiblical, it's dumb, right? Absolutely! But that's right! For those of you who don't believe me, I'm here to help you out. I'm going to share with you some recent criminal behavior and you tell me if they weren't a few bricks short of a load.

- Two men tried to pull the front off an ATM machine by running a chain from the machine to the bumper of their pickup truck. But instead of pulling off the front panel the machine, the machine pulled of the bumper off their truck. So naturally, they got scared and left the scene leaving behind their bumper, which guess what it still had on it? Their license plate number!

- One day, a company called "Guns For Hire" which stages gunfights for Western movies got a call from a 47 year old woman, who wanted to have her husband killed. That's right! She got 4-1/2 years in jail.

- A man walked into a Circle-K and put a $20 bill on the counter and asked for change. But when the clerk opened the cash drawer, the man pulled a gun and asked for all the cash in the register. So the man took the cash from the clerk and fled leaving the $20 bill on the counter. How much cash did he get the drawer? $15 dollars!

- Charged with speeding, a man from Florida made his appearance in court. Though he was going 90 in a 25mph zone, the man pleaded innocent. Why? Because, as he told the judge, he had taken a laxative and was obviously in a rush to get home.

- An elderly woman just left the store when upon returning to her vehicle, she found four strange males sitting in her car. So being frightened, the woman dropped her shopping bags and drew her handgun. She told the men that if they did not get out of the car, she would shoot them. So the four men ran off quickly, whereupon the lady got into the car but soon discovered her key wouldn't fit. That's when she realized her car was the identical one parked a few spaces down. So she drove to the police station to report story where the officer on duty, laughing hysterically, pointed to the other end of the counter where four pale men were reporting a car hijacking by a mean old lady with a gun.[1]

Now folks, I'd say that was some pretty dumb criminal behavior, how about you? But folks, believe it or not, do you know I've discovered some criminal behavior even dumber than that? And get this! It's actually being done by Christians. Can anybody guess what dumb criminal behavior that might be? Hey, that's right! It's when we act like we have practical amnesia! Talk about dumb criminal behavior!

Oh, we say we know who we are as the Church, but half the time, with our lips and with our lives, we act like we've forgotten who we are. It's not only detrimental in our walk with Christ. It keeps others from believing in Christ. Therefore, to avoid this atrocity of Christians living like they have practical amnesia by not knowing who they are, we're going to continue our study from the Word of God on the people of God entitled, "**The Character of the Church**."

We've already seen the first thing we need to know about the Church if we're going to stop acting like we have practical amnesia is that the Church is the Body of Christ. The second thing is that the Church is a Body of Brides. The third thing is that the Church is a Body of One. The fourth thing is that the Church is a Body of Hope. The fifth thing is that the Church is a Body of Joy. The sixth thing is that the Church is a Body of Love. In the last chapter we saw the seventh thing we need to know is that the Church is a Body of Peace. There we saw, believe it or not, how the American Church is actually behaving peaceless when the Bible says we should be peaceful. Why? Because we've forgotten how to be confident in God, content in God, and even courageous in God. Because of that, we're not only ceasing to be a Body of Peace, we're actually turning into a Body of fearful, worried, stressed-out people. I don't think that's the kind of Church Jesus came to die for, how about you?

People, believe it or not, do you know that's not the only thing we need to know about the Church if we're going to stop acting like we have practical amnesia? The **eighth thing** we need to know is **The Church is a Body of Strangers**. But hey, don't take my word for it. Let's listen to God's:

Hebrews 11:8-16 "By faith Abraham, when called to go to a place he would later receive as his inheritance, obeyed and went, even though he did not know where he was going. By faith he made his home in the promised land like a stranger in a foreign country; he lived in tents, as did Isaac and Jacob, who were heirs with him of the same promise. For he was looking forward to the city with foundations, whose architect and builder is God. By faith Abraham, even though he was past age – and Sarah herself was barren – was enabled to become a father because he considered him faithful who had made the promise. And so from this one man, and he as good as dead, came descendants as numerous as the stars in the sky and as countless as the sand on the seashore. All these people were still living by faith when they died. They did not receive the things promised; they only saw them and welcomed them from a distance. And they admitted that they were aliens and strangers on earth. People who say such things show that they are looking for a country of their own. If they had been thinking of the country they had left, they would have had opportunity to return. Instead, they were longing for a better country – a heavenly one. Therefore God is not ashamed to be called their God, for he has prepared a city for them."

Now folks, according to our text, the Bible is clear. The reason why Abraham lived in tents and roamed around all his life wasn't because he couldn't find a decent house to buy. No! What did the text say? He lived as a stranger on earth because he knew his real home wasn't on this earth, right? It was in heaven. Therefore, God was not ashamed to be called his God, right? How many of you would like God to say that about you?

Here's my point. Surely, we all know this, right? I mean, surely every Christian who has ever lived knows that the Church is to be a Body of Strangers, where people look at us and say, "Wow! Now there's a group of people who don't belong to this world. I mean, look at them. They are so strange! It's almost as if they have something better to live for." Surely we know that, right? Well, you'd think so, but we have some problems. Why? Because if you look at most Churches it doesn't look like we're strangers living for the things of heaven. Are you kidding? It looks like we've been seduced to live for this earth!

So, why in the world would Christians live for this earth when the Bible says we should be strangers living for heaven? Hey, great question. I'm glad you asked. It's pretty simple. The **first reason** why we're no longer strangers living for heaven is because we've been tricked into **Exchanging God's Dream for the American Dream**.

1 Corinthians 9:22-25 "I have become all things to all men so that by all possible means I might save some. I do all this for the sake of the gospel, that I may share in its blessings. Do you not know that in a race all the runners run, but only one gets the prize? Run in such a way as to get the prize. Everyone who competes in the games goes into strict training. They do it to get a crown that will not last; but we do it to get a crown that will last forever."

Now folks, according to our text, the Bible is clear. Paul became all things to all men and did whatever he had to do, just so he could do what? To share the gospel with everyone he met, right? Why did he do it? Did he do it because his Pastor told him to? Did he do it because his buddies were pressuring him into it? Did he do it because he was filling some sort of legalistic Christian quota? No! What did the text say? He did it to get a crown or reward that lasted forever, right? Why? Because he was fulfilling God's purpose or dream for his life, which by the way is His dream for all Christians. That is, to share the gospel with as many people as possible before we get to heaven.

People, the point is this. Surely the American Church knows this, right? I mean, surely we know that this world is a ticking time bomb that's one day going to blow up, right? Therefore we need to try to save as many people as we can before it's too late, right? People, are you kidding? Let's be honest! We don't live for God's dream. We live for the American dream. We don't live in hopes to take others with us to retire in heaven! We live in hopes to retire here on earth!

You might be thinking, "Well hey, wait a second. Aren't we supposed to be wise stewards and provide for our financial future the best as we can?" Of course we are people. But not at the expense of taking the time to share the gospel! Not if our only concern is to save and invest in the stock market instead of investing in saving people from hell! Besides people, have you ever stopped to think about what this American dream really is? In case you haven't, let me define it for you:

"Start studying when you're about seven years old, real hard. Then grow up and get a good job. Then from then on, get up at dawn every day, flatter your boss, crush your competition, and climb over backs of co-workers. Be the last one to leave every night. Squirrel away every cent. Avoid having a nervous breakdown and a premature heart attack and don't forget to get a face lift. Do this every day for thirty years, holidays and weekends included and by the time you're ready to retire you might have your money."[2]

Folks, I think the point is obvious. When you define it for what it is, in comparison to God's dream, the so-called American Dream is pretty stupid, don't you think? I mean stop and think about it. Who in their right mind would invest all their time and money in a world that is not only not their true home but is one day destined to blow up? I mean, isn't that strange? Of course it is, people! That's why God has called us to do whatever it takes like the Apostle Paul to save people from this dying world. Why? So one day they can join us in the ultimate retirement home, a place called heaven! People, when are we going to learn that the so-called American dream is nothing but a hellish trap that keeps us from saving others from hell! I didn't say that, this guy did:

"One day Pastor Richard Wurmbrand was speaking at a meeting in America after being exiled from Romania. While he was there, he manage to endure fourteen years of a brutal imprisonment, languishing in slave labor camps, and watched several of his friends being killed for being Christians. When the meeting ended, one of the people there asked him, 'Pastor, why is it that we don't have to deal with Communism here in America?'

Well, one would have expected him to say, 'It's because of your national heritage! Or it's because you haven't built or accepted a Communist government. Or because there are too many believers in your country to allow such a thing to happen.'

Yes, he could have responded like that and to a great extent, he would have been correct. But that was not his answer. Instead he replied, 'You don't have Communism here; you have something far worse. You have materialism!'"[3]

Now folks, why is it that a Christian from Communistic Russia can see dangers of materialism, but we in the American Church can't? I mean, don't you find it strange?

People, the point is this. If you don't want to live God's dream and instead live for the American dream, I guess that's your choice. But what you need to know is that it doesn't stop there! It's not only a stupid thing to do in your walk with Christ. It's a stumbling block for someone coming to Christ. Why? Because it's a no-brainer people! Think about it from the non-Christian's point of view. If retirement on earth is better than retirement in heaven, then why would I want to go there? Maybe heaven is here on earth? How many of you have heard that before? Gee, I wonder where they're getting it from?

Oh, but that's not all. The **second reason** why we're no longer strangers living for heaven is because we've been tricked into **Exchanging Treasures in Heaven for Trash on Earth**.

1 John 2:15-17 "Do not love the world or anything in the world. If anyone loves the world, the love of the Father is not in him. For everything in the world – the cravings of sinful man, the lust of his eyes and the boasting of what he has and does – comes not from the Father but from the world. The world and its desires pass away, but the man who does the will of God lives forever."

Now folks, according to our text, the Bible is clear. If you and I want to demonstrate that we really love God, what do we have to do? We not only start taking others with us to heaven, we what? We stop longing for the things of this world, right? Why? Because the things of this world are not only catering to our sinful flesh, they're nothing but trash! They cannot and will not last forever, right?

People, the point is this. Surely the American Church knows this, right? I mean, surely we know we need to spend our time storing up treasure in heaven because one day all we've accumulated on earth will be burned up like trash, right? People, are you kidding? Let's be honest! We don't live for treasure in heaven. We live for trash on earth. We don't get excited about our glorious surroundings in heaven! We get excited about the grand opening of a Home Depot!

You might be thinking, "What's wrong with having a few nice things in life. I mean, doesn't God want His children to enjoy life a little?"

Of course He does, people. But not at the expense of loving created things more than the Creator. Not if our only concern is to get more stuff instead of getting somebody saved! Besides people, have you ever stopped to think about how the average person lives just so they could get this trash on earth? Well, in case you haven't, let me define it for you:

"Our so-called American way of life is based upon people who are ready to spend money they don't have to buy things they don't need to impress people they don't know and who in the end, are people who don't care. The tragedy of all this is that it takes a lot of money to buy all of these things that nobody needs, and in order to get that money most of us neglect what is really important. We don't have time for meaningful relationships."

And might I add, "We don't have time to share the gospel." People, this is why when you define it for what it is, living for trash on earth is pretty stupid, don't you think? I mean stop and think about it. Who in their right mind would invest all their time and money in things that are one day destined to become trash? I mean, isn't that strange? Of course it is, people! But that's right! If you don't want to believe me, then maybe you should listen to this guy:

"E. Stanley Jones, talks about a fictional person who lived out a fantasy life. And all he had to do was think of it and poof! It happened. So this man, in a moment of time, sticks his hands in his pockets and leans back and imagines a mansion and poof! He has a fifteen-bedroom mansion, three stories with servants instantly available to wait upon his every need.

So he thought, 'Why, a place like that needs several fine cars.' So he again closes his eyes and imagines the driveway full of the finest wheels money can buy. And poof! There are several of the best vehicles instantly brought before his eyes. He is free to drive them himself or sit way back in the limousine with that Mafia glass wrapped around the rear, and have the chauffeur drive him wherever he wishes.

But soon there's no other place to travel so he comes back home and wishes for a sumptuous meal and poof! There's a meal in front of him with all of its mouth-watering aromas and beauty – which he eats alone.

And yet, there was something more he needed to find; happiness. Finally, he grows so terribly bored and unchallenged that he whispers to one of the attendants, 'I want to get out of this. I want to create some things again. I'd rather be in hell than be here.'

To which one of the servants replies quietly, 'Where do you think you are?'"[4]

People of God, when are we going to learn that living for the temporary things on earth not only leads to a hellish life, but once again it distracts from showing others how to get eternal life.

People, the point is this. If you don't want to live for treasure in heaven and instead live for trash on earth, I guess that's your choice. But what you need to know is that it doesn't stop there! It's not only a stupid thing to do in your walk with Christ. It's a stumbling block for someone coming to Christ. Why? Because it's a no-brainer people! Think about it from the non-Christians point of view. If trash on earth is better than the treasure of heaven, then why would I want to go there? Maybe heaven is here on earth? How many of you have heard that before? Gee, I wonder where they're getting it from?

Oh, but that's not all. The **third reason** why we're no longer strangers living for heaven is because we've been tricked into **Exchanging a Heavenly Reward for a Hellish Rat Race.**

Revelation 14:9,10,11,13 "If anyone worships the beast and his image and receives his mark on the forehead or on the hand, he too will drink of the wine of God's fury. And the smoke of their torment rises for ever and ever. There is no rest day or night for those who worship the beast and his image. Then I heard a voice from heaven say, Write: Blessed are the dead who die in the Lord from now on. They will rest from their labor, for their deeds will follow them."

Now folks, according to our text, the Bible is clear. If people worship the antichrist and his satanic world system, what do they get? They not only get God's wrath and torment but they get no rest for how long? Forever, right? But to those who give their lives to Christ and live for Him in the midst of this wicked world, what do they get? They not only get God's blessing and rest, but they get to do so for how long? Forever!

People, the point is this. Surely the American Church knows this, right? I mean, surely we know that if we live for this satanically inspired world system, we're not only going to miss out on God's rest but we're going to end up restless, right? People, are you kidding? Let's be honest! We don't live for God's rest in heaven, let alone on this earth. We live for a hellish rat race here on earth. For those of you who don't think we do, let me share this description of the so-called rat race life and you tell me if this isn't how the average person lives today, even Christians.

"This century's mad dash of innovation has produced the most frantic human era ever. We phone. We fax. We page. We e-mail. We race from one end of life to the other, rarely glancing over our shoulders.

Technology, mass media and a desire to do more, do it better and do it yesterday have turned us into a world of hurriers. Stop and smell the roses? No more. Instead, we have a world of 7-day diets, 24-hour news channels, 1-hour photo, 30-minute pizza delivery, 10-minute facials, 2-minute warnings, and Minute Rice.

Fast food. Fast computers. Fast cars in fast lanes. VCRs with 5 fast-forward settings. Sound bites and the rat race and instant coffee. Get rich quick. Live fast, die young, leave a good-looking corpse. Run on empty. Just do it.

Places to go, people to meet, planners to fill, files to download, bills to pay, planes to catch, frozen dinners to nuke, web sites to surf, kids to pick up, stress to manage, and speeding tickets to pay. "[5]

Now folks, I'd say when you look at it for what it is, the rat race is not only pretty restless, it's pretty stupid, don't you think?

You might be thinking, "Now wait a minute. You're being a little too harsh here. I mean, yeah okay, so I live for a retirement on earth more than a retirement in heaven and I live for things on earth more than treasure in heaven, and yeah, so I get a little restless living the rat race, but so what! Everyone does it. What's the big deal?" Big deal? I'll tell you what the big deal is. When you and I as Christians live like this, what are we doing? Believe it or not, we're giving the impression that the Church is a **bunch of mentally impaired people**! I didn't say that, this guy did:

"My brother Kevin thinks that God lives under his bed. At least that's what I heard him say one night. He was praying out loud in his dark bedroom, and I stopped outside his door to listen. 'Are you there, God?' he said. 'Where are you? Oh, I see. Under the bed.' And after this, I giggled and went off to my own room.

And it was there I began to ponder Kevin's unique perspective in life. He was born thirty years ago, mentally disabled as a result of difficulties during labor. I began to realize for the first time the different world Kevin lives in.

I don't think Kevin knows anything exists outside his world. He doesn't know what it means to be discontent. His life is simple. He will never know the entanglements of wealth or power, and he does not care what brand of clothing he wears or what kind of food he eats. In fact, he recognizes no differences in people and he treats each one like a friend.

His needs have always been met, and he never worries that one day they might not be. He simply trusts God. When he comes to Christ, he comes as a child. Kevin seems to know God – to really be friends with Him in a way

that is difficult for an 'educated' person to grasp. God seems like his
closest companion.

That's why in my moments of doubt and frustrations in my walk with God
I actually begin to envy Kevin's simple faith. And it is there I realize that
maybe Kevin's not the one with the handicap – maybe it's me."[6]

People of God, when are we ever going to learn that God not only
has a better plan for our lives, but He's got a better place for our lives? It's
called heaven and it's not here on earth! People, I'm telling you, the
longer we live like this, we're not only ceasing to be a Body of Strangers,
we're acting like a Body of Mentally Handicapped people! No wonder
people don't take us seriously when we talk about heaven!

People, if we can't stop playing Church instead of being the
Church then maybe it's time to get out of the Church. Why? Because
being a Christian is not a game. What we say and do literally affects the
eternal destiny of people around us. Therefore, it's high time we get rid of
our practical amnesia. We have to remember who we are! We're not a
bunch of mentally challenged earth-bound rats. Are you kidding? We are
the Church of Jesus Christ. We are a **Body of Strangers** on our way to
heaven!

Chapter Nine

A Body of Disciples

"One day, there was a middle-aged woman who had a heart attack and was taken to the hospital. While she was on the operating table, she had a near death experience. And so seeing God she asked Him if this was it.

And God said, 'No you have another 43 years, 2 months, and 8 days to live.'

So, upon recovery, the woman figuring since she had so much more time to live, she might as well make the most of it and live for herself. So she decided to stay in the hospital and have a facelift, liposuction, tummy tuck, and she even had someone come in and change her hair color.

But when she got out of the hospital after her last operation, she crossed the street and was hit and killed by an ambulance speeding back to the hospital.

So upon arriving back in front of God again she demanded, 'Hey God, I thought you said I had another 40 some years to go?'

And God replied, 'Oh, I'm sorry, I didn't recognize you.'"[1]

Now, that lady learned the hard way it doesn't pay to live for yourself, does it? Not at all! What happened? Changing her appearance not only cost her life again but it caused God to no longer recognize her, didn't it? But folks, believe it or not, do you know that lady's not the only one who has changed her appearance and is no longer recognizable to God? Believe it or not, so are many Christians. How? By walking around in life like we have practical amnesia! Talk about false appearances!

Oh, we say we know who we are as the Church, but half the time, with our lips and with our lives, we act like we've forgotten who we are. It's not only detrimental in our walk with Christ. It keeps others from believing in Christ. Therefore, to avoid this atrocity of Christians living like they have practical amnesia by not knowing who they are, we're going to continue our study from the Word of God on the people of God entitled, "**The Character of the Church**."

We've already seen the first thing we need to know about the Church if we're going to stop acting like we have practical amnesia is that the Church is the Body of Christ. The second thing is that the Church is a Body of Brides. The third thing is that the Church is a Body of One. The fourth thing is that the Church is a Body of Hope. The fifth thing is that the Church is a Body of Joy. The sixth thing is that the Church is a Body of Love. The seventh thing is that the Church is a Body of Peace. In the last chapter we saw the eighth thing we need to know is that the Church is a Body of Strangers. There we saw that even though the Bible says we need to be strangers on earth living for heaven, the American Church is actually behaving like we've been seduced into living for this earth. Why? Because we've exchanged God's dream for the American dream, treasure in heaven for trash on earth, and a heavenly reward for a hellish rat race. Because of that, we're not only ceasing to be a Body of Strangers, we're actually turning into a Body of mentally challenged earth-bound rats. I don't think that's the kind of Church Jesus came to die for, how about you?

People, believe it or not, do you know that's not the only thing we need to know about the Church if we're going to stop acting like we have practical amnesia? The **ninth thing** we need to know is **The Church is a Body of Disciples**. But hey, don't take my word for it. Let's listen to God's:

Matthew 28:16-20 "Then the eleven disciples went to Galilee, to the mountain where Jesus had told them to go. When they saw him, they worshiped him; but some doubted. Then Jesus came to them and said, All authority in heaven and on earth has been given to me. Therefore go and make disciples of all nations, baptizing them in the name of the Father and of the Son and of the Holy Spirit, and teaching them to obey everything I have commanded you. And surely I am with you always, to the very end of the age."

Now folks, according to our text, the Bible is clear. Jesus' plan for His Church wasn't just to have only twelve disciples, was it? How many did He want? A whole world full of disciples, right? For those of you who may not know, the word "disciple" comes from the Greek word, "mathetes" which means "a disciplined learner." Therefore, it's obvious that Jesus wanted all of His followers, not just the twelve disciples, to become disciplined learners, right?

Here's my point. Surely, we all know this, right? I mean, surely every Christian who has ever lived knows that the Church is to be a Body of Disciples, where people look at us and say, "Wow! Now there's a group of people who are followers of Christ. I mean, look at them. They're constantly learning about Jesus, pouring over His Words in the Bible, day in and day out! Surely we know that, right? Well, you'd think so, but we have some problems. Why? Because if you look at most Churches it doesn't look like we're learning all we can about our Lord Jesus Christ. Are you kidding? It looks like we're learning all we can about anything and everything but Jesus Christ!

So, why in the world do we do this? Why don't we Christians learn about Jesus when the Bible says we should be disciplined learners of Jesus? Hey, great question. I'm glad you asked. It's pretty simple. The

first reason why we're no longer disciples of Christ is because **We Study Trivial things Instead of the Truth**.

Romans 12:1-2 "Therefore, I urge you, brothers, in view of God's mercy, to offer your bodies as living sacrifices, holy and pleasing to God – this is your spiritual act of worship. Do not conform any longer to the pattern of this world, but be transformed by the renewing of your mind. Then you will be able to test and approve what God's will is – his good, pleasing and perfect will."

Now folks, according to our text, the Bible is clear. If we really want to show that we appreciate the goodness and mercy of God, what do we do? We stop living for ourselves and start living sacrificially for Jesus, right? Not only that, we stop thinking like this world and start renewing our minds with the truth of God, right? When we do that, what happens? We know how to live a life that is good and pleasing to God, right?

People, the point is this. Surely the American Church knows this, right? I mean, surely we know if we're ever going to be unbrainwashed from the lies of this world, let alone know God's will, then we have to be studying His truth, right? People, are you kidding? We don't learn all we can about the truth of God. We learn all we can about the trivia of man! Let's be honest! If we even get around to studying anything, what does it usually turn out to be? Maybe it's studying and memorizing the latest statistics on sports figures. Or maybe it's studying and compiling data on how to be physically fit. Or maybe with what little free time we do have it's studying and reading the latest best-selling novel. But in general, whatever we study, if we even get around to study, it's usually what? Anything and everything but God's truth, right?

People, don't misunderstand me. There's nothing inherently wrong with those activities. My point is this. If we only have a little time to study, why not make it the truth of God's Word instead of the trivia of man? Why? Because hello! Which one benefits your life the most? For instance, when tough times hit do you call upon the power of your trivial knowledge to help you out? Maybe you're having trouble in your marriage. Is this what you say, "Praise God I know who won the Super Bowl for the last ten years in a row! Whew! I think my marriage is going to be okay now!" Or maybe when your having financial difficulties do you say, "You know, times are really tough right now but praise God I know the fourteen reasons why I need vitamin C in my diet! I know my troubles are over now!" Or maybe your health is failing. Do you say, "Lord I'm in dire straits here. But I know I'm going to be healed because I've read every best-selling novel I can get my hands on!" Is that what we do? No people! We don't call upon the power of trivia of man. We call upon the power of God's truth! Therefore, if we never study God's truth, how in the world can we ever benefit from it? Not only that. How in the world can we call ourselves disciples of Christ when all we do learn about everything else but Christ?

People, the point is this. If you don't want to study God's truth and instead study only the trivia of man, I guess that's your choice. But what you need to know is that it doesn't stop there! It's not only a distraction in your walk with Christ. It could very well be a distraction for someone coming to Christ. Why? Because it's a no-brainer people! Think about it from the non-Christian's point of view. If Christians have no desire to study the Bible, then why would I want to study it? Apparently there's nothing good in there to apply to my life. How many of you have heard that before? Gee, I wonder where they're getting it from?

Oh, but that's not all. The **second reason** why we're no longer disciples of Christ is because **We Study Flippantly Instead of Consistently**.

Colossians 3:16 "Let the word of Christ dwell in you richly as you teach and admonish one another with all wisdom, and as you sing psalms, hymns and spiritual songs with gratitude in your hearts to God."

Now folks, according to our text, the Apostle Paul here is sharing with the Colossian Church what they're supposed to do every time they meet together. Notice it wasn't just singing and having a good ol' time.

What was it? It was to consistently teach or learn the Words of Christ so that it would what? So that it would dwell within us richly, right?

People, the point is this. Surely the American Church knows this, right? I mean, surely we know that if we're ever going to get to the point where God's truth dwells in us richly, we have to consistently take advantage of opportunities to learn, right? People, are you kidding? Let's be honest! We don't consistently come to Church services in order to learn. We flippantly come to Church services whenever we get the urge!

You might be thinking, "Now wait a minute man. I know I'm a little irregular in my attendance to Church services and Bible studies and I'm a frequent visitor of the Church of St. Mattress with Pastor I.B. Snoozing of the Bedside Sheets Assembly, but God knows my heart. He knows I'm still a faithful member of His." Oh really? Well, it just so happens I recently came across a letter written to a Pastor by one of these so-called faithful members and you tell me if in fact they were ever going to become a true disciple of Christ:

Dear Pastor,

You often stress attendance at Church services as being very important for a Christian. But I think a person has a right to miss now and then and be excused for the following reasons and the number of times indicated:

Christmas (Sunday before or after)............ 1
New Year's (Party lasted too long)............ 1
Easter (Get away for the holidays)............. 1
July 4th (National holiday)...................... 1
Labor Day (Need to get away)................... 1
Memorial Day (Visit hometown)................ 1
School closing (Kids need a break)............. 1
School opens (One last fling)................... 1
Family reunions (Mine and wife's)............. 2
Sleep late (Saturday night activities).......... 4
Deaths in family................................. 4

Anniversary (Second honeymoon)............ 1
Sickness (One for each family member)......5
Business trips (A must)........................ 3
Vacation (3 weeks)............................ 3
Bad weather (Ice, snow, rain, clouds).........6
Ball games..................................... 5
Unexpected company (Can't walk out)....... 5
Time changes (Spring ahead; fall back).......2
Special on TV (Super Bowl, etc.)..............3

So Pastor, that leaves only two Sundays per year. So, you can count on us to be in Church service on the fourth Sunday in February and the third Sunday in August unless providentially hindered.

Sincerely,

Faithful Member[2]

Now folks, I know this might be a tough question, but how many of you would say that so-called faithful member really was a faithful member? Yeah, who's kidding who, right?

People, please don't misunderstand me. This has nothing to do with Christian legalism. It has everything to do with Christian learning. For instance, we tell our kids if they're ever going to succeed in academic things they have to do what? They have to consistently be faithful in their studies right? Therefore, how much more is this true in spiritual things? And if we skip services and attend meetings only often enough to show we're interested but never enough to get involved in learning, how in the world are we ever going become disciples of Christ?

People, the point is this. If you don't want to study God's truth consistently and instead study it flippantly, I guess that's you're choice. But what you need to know is that it doesn't stop there! It's not only a delay in your walk with Christ. It could very well be delaying someone from coming to Christ. Why? Because it's a no-brainer people! Think about it from the non-Christian's point of view. If Christians have no desire to go to Church services to learn, then why would I want to? Apparently, there's no value in going. How many of you have heard that before? Gee, I wonder where they're getting it from?

Oh, but that's not all. The **third reason** why we're no longer disciples of Christ is because **We Study for Personal Gain Instead of Godly Gain**.

Philippians 2:20-22 "I have no one else like him, who takes a genuine interest in your welfare. For everyone looks out for his own interests, not those of Jesus Christ. But you know that Timothy has proved himself, because as a son with his father he has served with me in the work of the gospel."

Now folks, according to our text, the Bible is clear. If we want to be a loyal and genuine disciples-in-training like Timothy, what do we have to do? We not only stop looking out for ourselves but we start getting concerned with the things of Jesus, right? How do we do that? What did the text say? We devote ourselves to being educated Biblically, right?

People, the point is this. Surely the American Church knows this, right? I mean, surely we know that if we're ever going to be disciples of Christ, we have to be educating ourselves Biblically and not just secularly, right? People, are you kidding? Let's be honest! We don't study for godly gain. We study for personal gain! We don't study like Timothy to deliver God's message. We study so we can get delivered a bigger paycheck!

People when are we going to realize that the purpose of an education is not just to get a good job. The purpose of an education is to show yourself approved unto God! But that's right! If you think I'm being a little too radical, then maybe you should listen to this guy. Maybe he's got a better grip on the true purpose of an education:

"It becomes too easy to think that being a Christian is somebody who believes all the right stuff. I want you to believe in Jesus. I want you to

believe that He died on the cross for your sins. I want you to believe that He was resurrected. I want you to believe that He's here and now and wants to establish a personal relationship with you.

But listen to me. You can believe all the right stuff and not love Jesus and not love other people. As a matter of fact, the Church is filled with those who believe all the right stuff and don't know how to love.

Now, I know what you're going to say. You're saying, 'You're making Christianity too hard. I mean, my goodness. I didn't mind this belief stuff but you expect me to change the whole way in which I live?' Of course I do! That's what Christianity's about! It's about changing the whole way you live!

Maybe you don't like this Jesus. Maybe you don't like this Jesus who says, 'If any man would be my disciple, let him deny himself, take up his cross, and follow Me.' Maybe you don't like Him. That's okay. Reject Him! But for goodness sakes, do not call yourself a follower of Jesus if you're not!

The Jesus I talk to you about is radical, extremely radical, and He calls you to a whole new lifestyle, a dangerous lifestyle, and a threatening lifestyle. Because from the day you were a kid, they drilled into your head to fit into this American system. Your parents did it, the Church did it, and the school did it.

They said, 'Get a good education.' You talk about dropping out of school and they go crazy. And if you should ask why should I get a good education the answer is simple, 'If you get a good education you'll be able to get a good job. And a good job is one in which you earn a lot of money.'

Stop to think about how unchristian that is! You need to go to college. You need to get a good education. But the purpose of an education is not to make enough money to buy things! The purpose of an education is to equip yourself to serve others in the Name of Jesus!"

Now folks, I know what some of you might be thinking. "You know, that all sounds good and all but I think that guy's being a little too radical as well. I mean, we can't really be expected to live like that nowadays." Well, if you think that's a little too radical, then you're certainly not going to like the Founding Fathers of our Country. Let's see if they can remind us of what the true purpose of an education is:

- The first colleges formed in America (123 out of 126) were formed on Christian principles.

- Up until 1900 it was very rare to find a university president who was not and ordained clergyman.

- The New England Primer, America's first textbook and used for 210 years taught the alphabet like this: A – In Adam's fall we sinned all. C – Christ crucified for sinners died. Z – Zaccheus he did climb the tree our Lord to see.

- The 107 questions at the end of the New England Primer included questions like, "What offices does Christ execute as our Redeemer?" "How does Christ execute the office of a priest?" "What is required in the fifth commandment?" "What are the benefits which in this life do accompany or flow from justification, adoption, and sanctification?"

- George Washington made it crystal clear that American schools would teach Indian youths the "religion" of Jesus Christ and Congress assisted in doing so.

- In 1782, Congress had 10,000 bibles printed for use in schools.

- Dr. Benjamin Rush said, "The only means of establishing and perpetuating our republican forms of government is the universal education of our youth in the principles of Christianity by means of the Bible."

- Thomas Jefferson wrote the first plan of education for the city of Washington D.C. and adopted two textbooks, the Bible and Watts Hymnal, and hired clergymen to be the teachers.

- The 1854 edition of Webster's Dictionary had Biblical definitions, Bible verses, and Webster's own testimony of personally receiving Christ."

- America's first school was Harvard, founded in 1636 by Reverend John Harvard whose official motto was "For Christ and the Church." Harvard had several requirements which students had to observe, one of which was, "Let every scholar be plainly instructed and earnestly pressed to consider well, the main end of his life and studies is to know God and Jesus Christ, which is eternal life."[3]

Now folks, I'd say we've long forgotten the purpose of an education, how about you? In fact, I'd say it's our departure from it is what's truly radical! Gee, could this be the reason why we're seeing our country lose its Christian values and morals? Could it be because we're no longer educating ourselves in Christian values and morals?

You might be thinking, "Hey wait a minute. You're being a little too harsh here. I mean, yeah okay, so I study only trivial things instead of the truth and I only study flippantly instead of consistently and I only study for personal gain instead of godly gain, but so what! It only affects me!" Well, that's where you're wrong. You see, refusing to become a disciple of Christ has just as a dramatic affect as if you were to become one. Just ask Susanna Wesley:

"At the age of nineteen she became the wife of a minister named Samuel Wesley and was married forty-four years. During this time, they suffered illness, disease, poverty, and the death of many of their children. Through it all Susanna accepted it as the will of God and placed herself and her family in God's hands.

Susanna bore nineteen children nine of whom died as infants—including two sets of twins. One baby was accidentally smothered by a maid. Another was crippled for life in a tragic accident. But Susanna met her trials with the faith in God that she had learned when she was discipled as a child by her parents. You see, she was the youngest of twenty-five.

No matter the circumstances, Susanna was committed to caring for and discipling her family the best way possible. Though resources were limited, she started a daily school for her children. She said her purpose was exclusively 'the saving of their souls.' Because of that, the rigorous academics never took priority over instruction in God's Word.

Because Susanna wanted to develop a personal relationship with each one of her children, she scheduled a private appointment with each one every week for encouragement. It was these bonds of faith and love that helped them to survive their continual hardships.

Through it all Susanna Wesley remained a steadfast Christian who not only discipled herself through the Scriptures but her children as well. The results? Two of her sons, (maybe you've heard of them) John and Charles Wesley, won tens of thousands of souls to Jesus Christ. She could not have wished for more."[4]

Now folks, I'd say the world is a much better place because that one lady sacrificed to become a disciple of Christ, how about you? Can you imagine how many millions of people never would have been saved if Susanna Wesley refused to do so?

Here's the point. How many millions of people are never going to get saved and are going to go to hell because the American Church is refusing to become disciples of Christ? How many people will never know the joy of eternal salvation because we refuse to undergo a godly education?

People, if we can't stop playing Church instead of being the Church then maybe it's time to get out of the Church. Why? Because being a Christian is not a game. What we say and do literally affects the eternal destiny of people around us. Therefore, it's high time we get rid of our practical amnesia. We have to remember who we are! We're not a bunch of distracted people disinterested in Christ. Are you kidding? We are a bunch of disciplined learners in love with Christ. We're His Body. A **Body of Disciples**!

Chapter Ten

A Body of Servants

"As far as ham sandwiches go, it was perfection. It had a thick slab of ham, a fresh bun, crisp lettuce and plenty of that expensive, light brown, gourmet mustard. The corners of my mouth ached in anticipation as I carried it to the picnic table in our backyard.

As I picked it up with both hands ready to take a bite, I was stopped by my wife who appeared suddenly at my side and said, 'Can you hold the baby while I get my sandwich?'

I took my son and I balanced him between my left elbow and shoulder and was reaching again for the ham sandwich of perfection when I noticed a streak of mustard on my fingers. Since I had no napkin and since I love mustard, I licked it off.

The only problem was, it was not mustard. That's right! No man ever put a baby down faster than I did that day! In fact, it was the first and only time I have sprinted around with my tongue protruding from my face.

As I took a washcloth in each hand I did the sort of rapid fire routine that shoeshine boys do, only I did it on my tongue.

That's when my wife chimed in, 'Well, now you know why they call that mustard Poupon.'"[1]

Now how many of you are going to get a ham sandwich to eat while you're reading this chapter? In case you're wondering, no, I'm not the Father in that story! Here's my point. How many of you would say that man's encounter with his child left a bad taste in his mouth? But folks, believe it or not, do you know he's not the only one having a bad taste in his mouth from children? Believe it or not, this same scenario is happening all over our country every single day! How? By the children of God walking around in life like we have practical amnesia! Talk about leaving a bad taste in your mouth!

Oh, we say we know who we are as the Church, but half the time, with our lips and with our lives, we act like we've forgotten who we are. It's not only detrimental in our walk with Christ. It keeps others from believing in Christ. Therefore, to avoid this atrocity of Christians living like they have practical amnesia by not knowing who they are, we're going to continue our study from the Word of God on the people of God entitled, **"The Character of the Church."**

We've already seen the first thing we need to know about the Church if we're going to stop acting like we have practical amnesia is that the Church is the Body of Christ. The second thing is that the Church is a Body of Brides. The third thing is that the Church is a Body of One. The fourth thing is that the Church is a Body of Hope. The fifth thing is that the Church is a Body of Joy. The sixth thing is that the Church is a Body of Love. The seventh thing is that the Church is a Body of Peace. The eighth thing is that the Church is a Body of Strangers. In the last chapter we saw the ninth thing we need to know is that the Church is a Body of Disciples. There we saw that even though the Bible says were supposed to be disciples or disciplined learners of Christ, the American Church is discipling themselves all right. It's just that it's with anything and everything but Christ. Why? Because we study trivial things instead of the truth, we study flippantly instead of consistently, and we even study for personal gain instead of godly gain. Because of that, we're not only ceasing to be a Body of Disciples, we're actually turning into a Body of distracted people disinterested in Christ. I don't think that's the kind of Church Jesus came to die for, how about you?

People, believe it or not, do you know that's not the only thing we need to know about the Church if we're going to stop acting like we have practical amnesia? The **tenth** thing we need to know is **The Church is a Body of Servants**. But hey, don't take my word for it. Let's listen to God's:

Matthew 20:20-28 "Then the mother of Zebedee's sons came to Jesus with her sons and, kneeling down, asked a favor of him. What is it you want? he asked. She said, Grant that one of these two sons of mine may sit at your right and the other at your left in your kingdom. You don't know what you are asking, Jesus said to them. Can you drink the cup I am going to drink? We can, they answered. Jesus said to them, You will indeed drink from my cup, but to sit at my right or left is not for me to grant. These places belong to those for whom they have been prepared by my Father. When the ten heard about this, they were indignant with the two brothers. Jesus called them together and said, You know that the rulers of the Gentiles lord it over them, and their high officials exercise authority over them. Not so with you. Instead, whoever wants to become great among you must be your servant, and whoever wants to be first must be your slave – just as the Son of Man did not come to be served, but to serve, and to give his life as a ransom for many."

Now folks, according to our text, the Bible is clear. The disciples didn't have a clue as to what made for a great or successful Christian, did they? In fact, their cluelessness was causing trouble amongst them, wasn't it? Therefore, what did Jesus do? He had to correct them and tell them that a so-called super duper Christian was not one who had a high position and lots of people serving them. What did Jesus say? He said a super duper Christian was one who served lots of people just like Him, right?

Here's my point. Surely, we all know this, right? I mean, surely every Christian who has ever lived knows that the Church is to be a Body of Servants, where people look at us and say, "Wow! Look at those people! They have to be followers of Christ! They're constantly serving others, doing whatever it takes, sacrificing their lives just to help people in the name of Christ!" Surely we know that, right? Well, you'd think so, but we have some problems. Why? Because if you look at most Churches it doesn't look like we're doing all we can to serve others in the Name of Christ. Are you kidding? It looks like we're doing all we can to ensure others serve us no matter the price!

So, why in the world do we do this? Why do we Christians refuse to serve others in the Name of Christ when the Bible says we need to become servants like Christ? Hey, great question. I'm glad you asked. It's pretty simple. The **first reason** why we're no longer servants like Christ is because **We Think Serving is Done to Us.**

John 13:12-17 "When He had finished washing their feet, He put on His clothes and returned to His place. Do you understand what I have done for you? He asked them. You call me 'Teacher' and 'Lord,' and rightly so, for that is what I am. Now that I, your Lord and Teacher, have washed your feet, you also should wash one another's feet. I have set you an example that you should do as I have done for you. I tell you the truth, no servant is greater than his master, nor is a messenger greater than the one who sent him. Now that you know these things, you will be blessed if you do them."

Now folks, according to our text, the Bible is clear. If we really want to show we're followers of Christ and that He is our Master, what are we going to be doing? We're going to be doing the same thing the Master did, right? We're going to be stooping down and serving others even if it means washing their big ol' gnarly feet, right? The benefit for that was what? What did Jesus say? If we do that, we're going to have a what? A blessed life, right? How many of you would like to have a blessed life?

People, the point is this. Surely the American Church knows this, right? I mean, surely we know if we're ever going to have a blessed life let alone show the world we're really followers of Christ, we have to get busy serving others, right? People, are you kidding? Let's be honest! We don't think we need to live a life serving others. We think we need to live a life with others serving us! Why? Because we're not following Christ! We're following our culture!

People, whether you realize it or not, we live in a society today that scoffs at the idea of living a life of a servant. They don't say that's a blessed life. They call it a rotten life, a failure! They say a successful life is one that has enough money to do anything with their life and have others serve their every whim. But what did we read? Jesus says we're to sacrifice our lives in service to others just like Him! Why? Because it first of all protects us from becoming what I call Christian Brats! For instance, how many of you have ever gone to the store and you run across a little kid driving their Mom nuts saying, "I want this, I want that, give me this, give me that," and if they don't get what they want they kick or scream or throw a tantrum on the floor. When you see a kid like that, what do you want to do? You want to go over and lay hands on that child in a profound way, right? Why? Because they are acting like a selfish brat who thinks the whole world revolves around them, right? Therefore, if God's children walk around in life screaming "I want this, I want that, give me this, do that for me and if you don't serve me and meet my needs I'm going to throw a tantrum and leave," what would you call them? A brat in need of a spanking, right? How many of you know that God will spank His children?

Oh, but that's not all. The second reason Jesus says we need to be servants is because it protects us from not only being bratty Christians, but hypocritical Christians. For instance, can you imagine if you called the fire department and asked them to come help put out a fire and they shouted back, "Go get your garden hose and do it yourself! Don't you have water at your own house?" Or maybe you go to a restaurant and you ask the waitress to serve you some food and she yells, "Who do you think I am! Go back there and tell the cook yourself! What do you think I am your slave?" Or maybe you just got robbed and you flagged a policeman down and he said, "So what? What are you bothering me for? Can't you see I'm busy." Or can you imagine if a politician under a system of government that's of the people, by the people, and for the people, refused to listen to the people and do what they put him in office to do? No wait, they already do that! My point is this. In all of those cases, we expect those people to what? To sacrifice and serve the needs of others because that's what they're being paid to do, right? Therefore, if seeing a public servant refusing to serve the public ticks us off, how much more is God ticked off when His children are doing the same thing?

People, when are we going to learn that the Christian life is not asking what God can do for you! It's asking what you can do for God! We are to serve others just like Jesus did! Therefore, if a Christian refuses to serve others and follow in the footsteps of Christ, could it be that they're not really a follower of Christ? Kind of makes you wonder, doesn't it?

Oh, but that's not all. The **second reason** why we're no longer servants like Christ is because **We Think Serving is an Option for Us**.

Matthew 25:15-18,26,28,30 "To one he gave five talents of money, to another two talents, and to another one talent, each according to his ability. Then he went on his journey. The man who had received the five talents went at once and put his money to work and gained five more. So also, the one with the two talents gained two more. But the man who had received the one talent went off, dug a hole in the ground and hid his master's money. His master replied, You wicked, lazy servant! Take the talent from him and give it to the one who has the ten talents. And throw that worthless servant outside, into the darkness, where there will be weeping and gnashing of teeth."

Now folks, according to our text, the Bible is clear. There are two kinds of servants, aren't there? There are the good ones and the not so good ones, right? How do you know what a good one looks like? Simple. They take what God has invested in them and turn around and invest it in His kingdom, right? How do you know what a bad one looks like? Just as simple. They do just the opposite. They refuse to do anything, right? How many of you would say God is pleased with the bad ones? Yeah, usually the words wicked and lazy and weeping and gnashing of the teeth give it away!

People, the point is this. Surely the American Church knows this, right? I mean, surely we know that if we're going to live a life that is pleasing to God let alone one that demonstrates we're not phony baloney Christians, we're going to serve God no matter what, right? People, are you kidding? Let's be honest! We don't think serving is a command for us. We think it's an option! We don't serve consistently. We serve whenever it's convenient!

You might be thinking, "Now wait a minute man. I know I'm a little irregular in my service to God and I don't jump at the chance to do something for His kingdom all the time, let alone consistently, but God knows my heart. He knows I'm still a faithful servant of His." Oh really? Well, maybe we need to remind ourselves of the definition of faithful. Therefore, let's take a test. Let's see what makes something faithful:

- If your car started one out of three times, would you consider it faithful?

- If the paperboy skipped Mondays and Thursdays, would they be missed?

- If you didn't show up at work two or three times a month, would your boss call you faithful?

- If your refrigerator quit a day now and then, would you excuse it and say, "Oh, well, it works most of the time"?

- If your water heater greets you with cold water one or two mornings a week while you were in the shower, would it be faithful?

- If you miss a couple of mortgage payments in a year's time, would your bank say, "Oh, well, ten out of twelve isn't bad"?

- Therefore, if you miss worship services and attend meeting only often enough to show your interested but never enough to get involved, are you faithful?[2]

Now folks, I'd say being faithful requires a little bit of regularity, how about you? And if that kind of behavior won't fool a bank of man, do you really think we're fooling the Son of God? Therefore, if Christians live thinking service is an option instead of a command, could it be optional as to whether or not they really belong to Christ? Kind of makes you wonder, doesn't it?

Oh, but that's not all. The **third reason** why we're no longer servants like Christ is because **We Think Serving is Made for Us.**

Acts 20:34-35 "You yourselves know that these hands of mine have supplied my own needs and the needs of my companions. In everything I did, I showed you that by this kind of hard work we must help the weak, remembering the words the Lord Jesus himself said: It is more blessed to give than to receive."

Now folks, according to our text, the Bible is clear. We Christians must not only work to meet our needs but the needs of the who? The needs of the weak, right? Why? Because what did Jesus say? It is more blessed to give than to what? Than to receive, right?

Here's my point. Surely the American Church knows this, right? I mean, surely we know that if we're ever going to receive the blessings of God then we have to give away our lives in service to the weak, right? People, are you kidding? Let's be honest! We don't use God's gifts in service to others. We use God's gifts in service to us! We don't apply our skills and talents for the weak and downhearted. We apply them to get a big house and Ferrari!

People, in my opinion, this is precisely where the majority of the American Church is. Herein lies our biggest problem! You see, even when we realize that serving is not to be done to us, nor is it an option for us, we can still blow it! How? By taking our God-given gifts for the service of others and use them to serve only us!

To show you how easy this happens to Christians, I'm going to share with you two stories of two Christians and I want you to rate in your mind, using a scale from one to ten, how well they were using their God-given gifts for the service of others:

"I had a young student, and one time I took him with me to Haiti. I took him up to a medical center in the northern part of the country. I showed him a hospital where seven hundred people had lined up that morning for medical care. There was only one doctor and two nurses.

They only could take care of a hundred people. The other six hundred were turned away and when my student saw that he said, 'Doc, I'm going to go back and I'm going to complete my education and become a doctor and come back here to serve these people. That's my dream. That's the vision that God gave me.'

Well, I met him in New York last year and he's a doctor but he's not taking care of people in Haiti. Do you know what he's doing? Cosmetic surgery on women. Please, sometimes that's necessary but for the most part, what he is doing is a sheer absurdity.

But you see, there's a lot of money to made in doing cosmetic surgery for women. Much more than saving lives in Haiti! And so a dream was vanquished. A vision was obliterated."

Okay, I know it's going to be a tough decision, but think of that scale from one to ten and in your mind make a note as to what score you would give that guy on our Christian servant scale. Got it? Okay, now let's try servant number two:

"I had another student. His name is Brian Stevenson. He graduated from Eastern top of the class. He went to Harvard law school and graduated again from the top of his class. A young, handsome, brilliant, articulate African American man.

Have you any idea what a top graduate of Harvard law school is able to earn with a firm? A quarter of a million dollars? Easily. Do you know what he is doing? He's living in a one room flat in Montgomery Alabama. And every morning he gets up and goes down to the jailhouse and defends the men and women on death row for free!

Why? Because he said it has nothing to do with the death penalty. It has to do with this. We have two kinds of law in this country. One kind of law for the rich and the powerful and another kind of law for the poor and the oppressed. He said that we don't put criminals to death in America. We put poor people to death in America.

Why? Because the poor have no one to speak for them. Then he paused and said, 'Except in Montgomery Alabama. Because in Montgomery Alabama, Doc, I speak for the poor. And Doc, I'm good!'

Oh, Brian, you don't know how good you are! A young man who would not sell out to the system. A young man who had a dream and a vision that God had called him to do something significant with his life!"

Now folks, I know this might be a big surprise, but which one of those guys would you say scored higher on the servant scale? It's kind of obvious, isn't it? Now let me ask you one more question. Ask yourself, right now, with the way you've been living your Christian life, where would you be on that scale? Are you serving Christ or are you serving yourself?

You might be thinking, "Hey wait a minute. You're being a little too harsh here. I mean, yeah okay, so I think serving is done to me instead of others and I think serving in general is an option not a command and yeah I haven't been using my God given gifts for others but so what! It only affects me!" Well, that's where you're wrong. You see, sometimes refusing to become a servant really is a matter if life and death, like this lady learned:

"One day a Mother received a phone call from her son who had been away for a long time serving in the Vietnam War. And after the pleasant gestures were over the son asked his Mom, 'Mom I can come home in a couple of weeks but I was wondering if I could bring a friend with me?'

The Mother replied, 'Well, sure you can bring a friend.'

But the son continued, 'Well, you see, there's something you need to know Mom. You see, my friend was hurt pretty bad during the war and he's going to need a little bit if care. He has only one eye, one arm, and one leg.'

And his Mom hesitated a bit but replied, 'Well, I guess it would be okay for a couple of weeks or so.' But her son pressed one more time, 'But Mom, it wouldn't be for a few weeks. It would be forever. You see, Mom, he has no family. He has nobody to take care of him.'
Well at this the Mother explained that this would seriously disrupt their life and it wouldn't be very convenient with their lifestyle and all, and besides what would people think.

So the son paused for a moment but then simply replied, "Okay Mom. But whatever happens, just know that I love you very very much."

And it just so happened that two weeks later, the Mother got another phone call. Only this one informed her that her son had jumped out of a hospital window and killed himself. And so this mother, confused and bewildered, in a matter of days, found herself having to say goodbye to her son at a funeral service instead of welcoming him back home.

As hard as that was, nothing could have prepared her for what she was about to encounter. You see, as she approached the casket to say goodbye, she saw that her son had only one eye, one arm, and one leg.

As she cried out in utter despair, she realized that it was her son who was the friend in need of someone to love and serve him, but now it was too late!"[3]

Now folks, I have a sneaking suspicion that Mother kind of regretted not being willing to be a servant to others, how about you? Here's the point. How many millions of people will die and will go to hell because the American Church is likewise unwilling to be servants of Christ?

People, if we can't stop playing Church instead of being the Church then maybe it's time to get out of the Church. Why? Because being a Christian is not a game. What we say and do literally affects the eternal destiny of people around us. Therefore, it's high time we get rid of our practical amnesia. We have to remember who we are! We're not a bunch of selfish self-centered servants of man. Are you kidding? We are a bunch of submitted servers of God, just like Christ. We're His Body. A **Body of Servants!**

Chapter Eleven

A Body of Rebels

Hey, how many of you guys have ever run across somebody whose elevator didn't quite go up to the top or they were a few peas short of a casserole or their wheel was a spinning, but the ol' hamster was dead? You know what I'm saying? Well hey, that's right! For those of you who haven't had the privilege, I'm here to help you out. I'm going to share with you some actual quotes from these kinds of people, and I want you to tell me if their cheese hasn't done slid off their cracker!

- Miss Alabama of the Miss USA contest was asked, "If you could live forever, would you and why?" Her answer: "I would not live forever, because we should not live forever, because if we were supposed to live forever, then we would live forever, but we cannot live forever, which is why I would not live forever."

- Mariah Carey said, "Whenever I watch TV and see those poor starving kids all over the world, I can't help but cry. I mean I'd love to be skinny like that but not with all those flies and death and stuff."

- Matt Lauer on NBC's Today Show said, "Researchers have discovered that chocolate produces some of the same reactions in the brain as marijuana. The researchers also discovered other similarities between the two, but can't remember what they are."

- Brooke Shields said as spokeswoman for a federal anti-smoking campaign, "Smoking kills. If you're killed, you've lost a very important part of your life."

- Marion Barry, Mayor of Washington, DC said, "Outside of the killings, Washington has one of the lowest crime rates in the country."

- Hillary Clinton commented on the release of subpoenaed documents, "I'm not going to have some reporters pawing through our papers. We are the president."

- Rita Mae Brown said, "The statistics on sanity are that one out of every four Americans is suffering from some form of mental illness. Think of your three best friends. If they are okay, then it's you."

- Richard Gere said, "I know who I am. No one else knows who I am. If I was a giraffe and somebody said I was a snake, I'd think 'No, actually I am a giraffe.'"

- Kate Moss about her new book, "To say this book is about me which is the main reason I was uncomfortable, me, me, me, me, me, is ridiculous. This book is not about me." The name of her book? *Kate: The Kate Moss Book.*"

- Donald Rumsfeld said, "Reports that say that something hasn't happened are always interesting to me, because as we know, there are known knowns; there are things we know we know. We also know there are known unknowns; that is to say we know there are some things we do not know. But there are also unknown unknowns – the ones we don't know we don't know."[1]

Now folks, I'd say those people probably don't have all their cornflakes in one box? But folks, believe it or not, do you know they're not the only ones forgetting to engage their brains before speaking? Believe it or not, the American Church is doing the same thing! How? By walking around in life like we have practical amnesia! Talk about brainless behavior!

Oh, we say we know who we are as the Church, but half the time, with our lips and with our lives, we act like we've forgotten who we are. It's not only detrimental in our walk with Christ. It keeps others from believing in Christ. Therefore, to avoid this atrocity of Christians living like they have practical amnesia by not knowing who they are, we're going to continue our study from the Word of God on the people of God entitled, "**The Character of the Church**."

We've already seen the first thing we need to know about the Church if we're going to stop acting like we have practical amnesia is that the Church is the Body of Christ. The second thing is that the Church is a Body of Brides. The third thing is that the Church is a Body of One. The fourth thing is that the Church is a Body of Hope. The fifth thing is that the Church is a Body of Joy. The sixth thing is that the Church is a Body of Love. The seventh thing is that the Church is a Body of Peace. The eighth thing is that the Church is a Body of Strangers. The ninth thing is that the Church is a Body of Disciples. In the last chapter we saw the tenth thing we need to know is that the Church is a Body of Servants. There we saw that even though the Bible says were supposed to be serving others just like Christ, the American Church is serving all right, they're serving themselves instead of Christ! Why? Because we think serving is done to us, that serving is up to us, and we think serving is made for us. Because of that, we're not only ceasing to be a Body of Servants, we're actually turning into a Body of selfish self-centered servants of man. I don't think that's the kind of Church Jesus came to die for, how about you?

People, believe it or not, do you know that's not the only thing we need to know about the Church if we're going to stop acting like we have practical amnesia? The **eleventh thing** we need to know is **The Church is a Body of Rebels**. But hey, don't take my word for it. Let's listen to God's:

Romans 12:1-2 "Therefore, I urge you, brothers, in view of God's mercy, to offer your bodies as living sacrifices, holy and pleasing to God – this is your spiritual act of worship. Do not conform any longer to the pattern of this world, but be transformed by the renewing of your mind. Then you will be able to test and approve what God's will is – his good, pleasing and perfect will."

Now folks, according to our text, the Bible is clear. If we really appreciate God's mercy in saving us from our sins by sacrificing His Son, what are we going to do? We're going to sacrifice our lives right back at Him, right? The question is, "How do we know when we're doing that?" Well, what did the text say? We know we're sacrificing our lives back unto God when we're no longer conforming our lives unto to this world, right? And what do we usually call somebody who refuses to conform to something? We call them a what? A rebel, right? Therefore, God is giving us divine permission to be what? Rebels for Jesus, right? Exactly!

Here's my point. Surely, we all know this, right? I mean, surely every Christian who has ever lived knows that the Church is to be a Body of Rebels, where people look at us and say, "Wow! Look at those people! They have to be followers of Christ! They absolutely refuse to have anything to do with this world's wickedness. In fact, they'll face any threat and take any persecution just to stand up for God's truth." Surely we know that, right? Well, you'd think so, but we have some problems. Why? Because if you look at most Churches it doesn't look like we're Christian rebels with a cause. Are you kidding? We look like worldly conformists without a cause!

So, why in the world do we do this? Why do we Christians no longer rebel against this world and instead conform to this world? Hey, great question. I'm glad you asked. It's pretty simple. The **first reason** why we're no longer rebels for Christ is because **We've lost Our Saltiness**.

Matthew 5:13 "You are the salt of the earth. But what good is salt if it has lost its flavor? Can you make it salty again? It will be thrown out and trampled underfoot as worthless." (NLT)

Now folks, according to our text, the Bible is clear. The reason why God doesn't take us to heaven the moment we get saved is why? Because He's got a purpose for our lives before we get there, right? And what was that purpose? Are we called to be the paprika of the earth, the pepper of the earth, or even the pork-rub of the earth? No! What was it? We're called to be the preservative or the salt of the earth, right?

People, the point is this. Surely the American Church knows this, right? I mean, surely we know if our society is ever going to be preserved from absolute wickedness then the Church has got to stand for God's absolute righteousness, right? People, are you kidding? Let's be honest! We don't look like we're salt shakers preserving this earth. We look like sin shakers partying with the earth! Why? Because we're no longer rebels for Christ. We're no longer standing up for God's moral hierarchy of laws. We've conformed to the moral relativism of man.

For those of you who may not know, relativism is the belief where there is no right or wrong. Maybe you've heard the saying, "Whatever's true for you is true for you, and whatever's true for me is true for me." Have you heard that before? Of course, it's all over the place. Folks, what most people don't know is relativism is not just sinful, it's dumb! For instance, if there's no right and wrong then what's the difference between an Adolph Hitler and a Billy Graham? Who are we to judge? Or what's the difference between a psychopath murderer and a soccer Mom? Well, actually, those ladies can get pretty violent at the games, especially if their kids are losing, but that's not my point! My point is this. If there is no right or wrong people, stop and think about it! Then all forms of behavior must be acceptable, be it murder, adultery, or abortion, rape, etc., right? That would be dumb to think like that, right? Slightly!

Oh, but that's not all! What's really dumb is that the moment you say there are no absolutes, you just made a what? An absolute statement!

Hello! I'd say somebody's a few peas short of a casserole, how about you? In fact folks, even Abraham Lincoln pointed out about the stupidity of relativism:

"Abraham Lincoln was trying to make a point in a debate but his opponent was unconvinced and stubborn. So, Lincoln tried another tactic. He said to the man, 'Well, let's see now. How many legs does a cow have?'

The disgusted reply came back, 'Well, four, of course.'

Lincoln agreed and said, 'That's right. Now, suppose you call the cow's tail a leg. How many legs would the cow have?'

The opponent replied confidently, 'Why, five, of course.'

Lincoln came back, 'Now, that's where you're wrong. Calling a cow's tail a leg doesn't make it a leg!'"[2]

Now, if calling a cow's tail a leg could make it a leg, I personally would be excited. I mean, stop and think about it. That's just more meat to eat off of that baby, right? The point is this. Even if I did that, it wouldn't change a thing, would it? Not at all! For some goofy reason it doesn't keep us from trying! One man shares how people today are actually trying to call a cow's tail a leg, if you will, by redefining our morality. It's the same procedure:

"What our Founding Fathers referred to as drunkenness because of their Christian heritage, we now call alcoholism and deem it a social disease, rather than a sin.

What the Law/Word called sodomy, we now call an alternative life style. Pornography is a perversion that brings death to a nation and yet we call it adult entertainment.

*What our Founding Fathers called immorality, we now call the new
morality; what the law called adultery or fornication, we now call
stepping out or fooling around; and what the Law called abhorrent social
behavior (like stealing or filthy language), we now call abnormal social
development or anti-social behavior.* "[3]

Now folks, I don't think God's going to change His mind on sin
just because we've changed the name of sin, hello! That's kind of dumb,
isn't it? Oh, but that's not all! Relativism is not only dumb, it's flat out
dangerous!

Isaiah 5:20 "Woe to those who call evil good, and good evil; Who
substitute darkness for light and light for darkness; Who substitute bitter
for sweet and sweet for bitter!"

Now folks, I'd say we're actually living in a time when people are
doing just that. I mean, correct me if I'm wrong but are not people today
calling evil good and substituting darkness for light? The point is this.
What did God say about that kind of behavior? Did He say you're headed
for incredibly wild times? Or did He say you're headed for woeful times?
Woeful, right? That's right! For those of you down south, He's not talking
about riding a horsey. He's talking about some really bad times.

So what do we do? Is it too late? Is there any hope? Is it all over
for us? No people! Praise God, He's faithful. He's given us the antidote!
This antidote has the ability to preserve our country just in the nick of
time! Can anybody guess what that antidote is? Hey, that's right! It's you
and me the Church! We're the salt, the preservative of the earth standing
up for God's absolute righteousness in order to protect us from absolute
wickedness, right?

Here's the point. Surely, that's what we're doing, right? I mean,
surely we're standing up for God's absolute truth no mater what, right? I
mean, after all, we're Christians! Well, first of all, stop calling me Shirley,
but secondly, no people, we're not. For those of you who may not believe

me, let's take a look what the average Christian is actually standing for these days. Let's check the salt content:

1. 55% of Christians say the Bible has errors in it.
2. 50% of Christians say there is no absolute truth.
3. 47% don't have a commitment to the Christian faith as a top priority.
4. 58% don't have being active in a local church as one of their top goals in life.
5. 35% of Christians say that to get by in life these days, sometimes you have to bend the rules for your own benefit.
6. 65% say that satan does not exist.
7. 29% say that when Jesus lived on earth, He committed sins like everybody else.
8. 25% agree that it doesn't matter what faith you follow because all paths lead to heaven.
9. 49% of Pastors no longer have a Biblical worldview.
10. 93% of Christians no longer have a Biblical worldview.[4]

Now folks, I'd say we're losing our saltiness, how about you? In fact, I'd say if something doesn't turn around quick, we're in a heap of trouble! That's exactly what Charles Spurgeon said:

"We have come to a turning-point in the road. If we turn to the right, maybe our children and our children's children will go that way; but if we turn to the left, generations yet unborn will curse our names for having been unfaithful to God and to His Word."[5]

Whoa! Wait a second! Could our behavior today really affect the next generation? Uh, slightly! But hey, if you don't want to listen to Charles Spurgeon, maybe you should listen to modern historians. People of God, right now, we the Church are in what Historians are calling the terminal generation. In other words, unless this generation of Christians repents and turns around, our once Christian nation is going down! Why? Because what did Jesus say? If we lose our saltiness, we've not only lost our usefulness, but what? We'll eventually end up where? In the garbage, right? Therefore, could this be the reason why our country is filled with garbage? Could it be that the problem isn't so much with the American people as it is the American Church losing its saltiness? Kind of makes you wonder, doesn't it?

Oh, but that's not all. The **second reason** why we're no longer rebels for Christ is because **We've Lost our Brightness**.

Matthew 5:14-16 "You are the light of the world – like a city on a hilltop that cannot be hidden. No one lights a lamp and then puts it under a basket. Instead, a lamp is placed on a stand, where it gives light to everyone in the house. In the same way, let your good deeds shine out for all to see, so that everyone will praise your heavenly Father."

Now folks, according to our text, the Bible is clear. The second reason why we don't go to heaven the moment we get saved is why? It's because God has another purpose for our lives, right? What did it say? We're not just the salt of the earth. We're the what? We're the light of the earth! When we live bright and holy lives for God, what does it do? It exposes and repels the darkness of the world, right?

The point is this. Surely the American Church knows this, right? I mean, surely we know if we're ever going to beat back society's wicked behavior, it's not just believing the truth, it's by obeying the truth, right? People, are you kidding? Let's be honest! We don't look like we're shining for Jesus for all the world to see. We look like we're sinning with this world in hopes that God doesn't see! Why? Because people whether you realize it or not, relativism not only effects your beliefs, it causes you to lose your saltiness. It affects your behavior, causing you to lose your brightness! For those of you who may not believe me, let's take a look at current Christian behavior and you tell me if relativism hasn't affected it just a little bit. Let's check out our current light show:

1. 42% of Christians believe that it is more important to achieve success or win acceptance from other people than to please God.
2. 49% of Christians don't have a problem with the distribution of pornography.

3. Darryl, 17 – "Kids at school are pressuring me and my girlfriend to have sex. I want to wait until marriage, but I worry about how this makes me look."
4. Kendra, 14 – "I know the Bible says you can't have sex before marriage. But why can't you, if you're in love with the person? It doesn't feel wrong."
5. 39% of Christians say it's okay for couples to live together before marriage.
6. Christians are now more likely than non-Christians to get divorced. (27% vs. 24%).
7. 33% of Christians say homosexuality is okay.
8. A United Methodist minister has written a book on Jesus that claims that Jesus not only condoned homosexual relationships, but that Jesus Himself was involved in one. The minister has not been reprimanded by his denomination.
9. 4% of Christians and 3% of non-Christians said they had consulted a medium or spiritual advisor within the past month.
10. Nearly 64% thought that it was perfectly fine to be a Wiccan. (THAT'S A WITCH!)[6]

Now folks, I'd say we're losing our brightness, how about you? In fact, I'd say if something doesn't turn around quick, we're in a heap of trouble! That's exactly what this man said:

"In the 1830s, a Frenchman named Alexis deTocqueville came to America in order to find out what made this country so great. Here's what he said.

'I sought for the greatness and genius of America in her commodious harbors and her ample rivers, and it was not there; in her fertile fields and boundless prairies, and it was not there; in her rich mines and her vast world commerce, and it was not there.'

He said, 'Not until I went to the Churches of America and heard her pulpits aflame with righteousness did I understand the secret of her genius and power.

He said, 'America is great because America is good. And if America ever ceases to be good, America will cease to be great.'"[7]

What? Could our behavior today really affect the outcome of our country? Uh, slightly! That's why I've said it before and I'll say it again! We don't need revival in America. We need revival in the American Church!!! Why? Because what did Jesus say? If we lose our brightness, we're not only losing our purpose, but what? We'll eventually end up in a godless world. Therefore, could this be the reason why our country is looking so ungodly? Could it be that the problem isn't so much with American people as it is the American Church losing its brightness? Kind of makes you wonder, doesn't it?

You might be thinking, "Hey wait a minute. You're being a little too harsh here. I mean, yeah okay, so maybe I've lost a little bit of my saltiness and I don't stand for God's truth. And yeah, maybe my behavior has started to lose its brightness as well, but come on! You're being an alarmist! You're blowing this way out of proportion, pal!" Oh really? Well, I tell you what. I want you to imagine that kind of thinking in this kind of scenario and then tell me if I'm really overreacting:

"Can you imagine if you we're at a Church prayer meeting (That would be hard to imagine, wouldn't it?) when somebody runs in from the parking lot yelling, 'Turn on a radio, turn on a radio!' While you listen you discover that a mystery flu is sweeping across the country killing millions of people. Doctors are working around the clock trying to find an antidote but nothing is working!

Just when all hope seems lost, the news comes out. The code has been broken. A vaccine can be made. But it's going to take the blood of somebody who hasn't been infected yet.

So, everyone is asked to do one simple thing. Go to your local hospital and have your blood taken. Sure enough, you and your family go down with thousands of others to get your blood taken.

Then all of a sudden, a doctor comes running out of the hospital screaming, waving a clipboard and yelling a name and you can't believe your ears. Your son tugs on your jacket and says, 'Daddy, that's me.'

Before you know it, they've grabbed your boy while saying, 'It's okay. Your son's blood is perfect. We can make the vaccine.' As the word begins to spread across the parking lot, thousands of people erupt with joy!

That's when a doctor comes over, no longer smiling like the rest and says, 'We had no idea it would be a little child. We weren't prepared. I'm sorry sir, we're going to need all of his blood.' You stammer and hesitate as the doctor continues, 'We're talking about the whole world, sir. Please sign this consent form. We need it all!'

In numb silence, you do. Then they say, 'Would you like to have a moment with him before we begin?' Can you imagine walking back to that room with your son on a table saying, 'Daddy? Mommy? What's going on?' Before you can answer, the doctor comes back in and says, 'I'm sorry, we have to get started! People all over the world are dying.'

Now can you imagine having to leave? Can you imagine walking out while your son is saying, 'Daddy? Mommy? Why are you leaving me?'

Then can you imagine the very next week after it's all over when they are having the ceremony to honor your son's life that some people actually sleep through it? Some don't even come because they want to go to the lake? Some folks do come but they have a phony smile just 'pretending' to care.

Can you imagine that? I mean, wouldn't you want to jump up and scream, 'MY SON DIED FOR YOU! DON'T YOU EVEN CARE?' Can you imagine that?"[8]

Now folks, can you imagine people really acting like that? I mean, can you imagine people really being that callous to the sacrifice of that man's only son? Can you imagine how horrible that would be? Then, how much more horrible is it when we do the very same thing? Didn't God give us the life of His Son? Didn't Jesus shed His blood to save the world from sin? Therefore, if we don't care enough to stand up for God's truth, let alone live it, how are we being any different than those people? Aren't we being just as callous? Aren't we being just as ungrateful? How horrible is that?

People, if we can't stop playing Church instead of being the Church then maybe it's time to get out of the Church. Why? Because being a Christian is not a game. What we say and do literally affects the eternal destiny of people around us. Therefore, it's high time we get rid of our practical amnesia. We have to remember who we are! We're not a bunch of saltless dark conformists of man. Are you kidding? We're a bunch of righteous revolutionaries on fire for Christ! We're His Body. A **Body of Rebels!**

Chapter Twelve

A Body of Worshippers

"One day a wife was busy frying eggs, when her husband came home. As soon as he walked into the kitchen, he immediately started yelling,

'CAREFUL HONEY!!! CAREFUL!!! USE MORE OIL!!! TURN THEM!!! TURN THOSE EGGS NOW!!! WE NEED MORE OIL!!! HONEY THEY'RE GOING TO STICK!!! CAREFUL!!! CAREFUL!!! TURN THEM!!! TURN THEM!!! HURRY UP!!! ARE YOU CRAZY!!!! THE OIL IS GOING TO SPILL!!! THE SALT!!! THE SALT!!! USE MORE SALT!!! USE THE SALT!!!!'

At this, the wife got completely outraged and said, 'What in the world is wrong with you? Don't you think I know how to fry an egg?'

The husband calmly replied, 'Well, of course, but now you know how I feel when you ride next to me in the car!'"[1]

Now, how many of you guys can identify with that story? Oh, come on you chickens! That's right! For you brave folks out there, the point is this. Backseat drivers are pretty annoying, aren't they? But folks, believe it or not, do you know I've discovered something even more annoying than back seat drivers? Uh huh, I really have. Can anybody guess what it is? That's right! It's called backsliding Christians walking around acting like they have practical amnesia! Talk about annoying behavior!

Oh, we say we know who we are as the Church, but half the time, with our lips and with our lives, we act like we've forgotten who we are. It's not only detrimental in our walk with Christ. It keeps others from believing in Christ. Therefore, to avoid this atrocity of Christians living like they have practical amnesia by not knowing who they are, we're going to continue our study from the Word of God on the people of God entitled, "**The Character of the Church**."

We've already seen the first thing we need to know about the Church if we're going to stop acting like we have practical amnesia is that the Church is the Body of Christ. The second thing is that the Church is a Body of Brides. The third thing is that the Church is a Body of One. The fourth thing is that the Church is a Body of Hope. The fifth thing is that the Church is a Body of Joy. The sixth thing is that the Church is a Body of Love. The seventh thing is that the Church is a Body of Peace. The eighth thing is that the Church is a Body of Strangers. The ninth thing is that the Church is a Body of Disciples. The tenth thing is that the Church is a Body of Servants. In the last chapter we saw the eleventh thing we need to know is that the Church is a Body of Rebels. There we saw that even though the Bible says were supposed to be rebelling against this world system, the American Church is conforming to this world system! Why? Because we've not only lost our saltiness, we've lost our brightness. Because of that, we're not only ceasing to be a Body of Rebels, we're actually turning into a Body of saltless, dark conformists of man. I don't think that's the kind of Church Jesus came to die for, how about you?

People, believe it or not, do you know that's not the only thing we need to know about the Church if we're going to stop acting like we have practical amnesia? The **twelfth thing** we need to know is **The Church is a Body of Worshippers**. But hey, don't take my word for it. Let's listen to God's:

Matthew 22:34-39 "Hearing that Jesus had silenced the Sadducees, the Pharisees got together. One of them, an expert in the law, tested him with this question: Teacher, which is the greatest commandment in the Law? Jesus replied: Love the Lord your God with all your heart and with all your soul and with all your mind. This is the first and greatest commandment. And the second is like it: Love your neighbor as yourself. All the Law and the Prophets hang on these two commandments."

Now folks, according to our text, the Bible is clear. The greatest way we can show our love to God is how? It's to keep the greatest commandment, right? Which was what? To love the Lord your God with all your heart, with all your soul, and all your mind, right? Notice it wasn't loving or worshipping God whenever we feel like it, or whenever we get around to it, or whenever it's convenient, or whenever it's popular. No folks! What did it say? It's with everything we have, right?

Here's my point. Surely, we all know this, right? I mean, surely every Christian who has ever lived knows that the Church is to be a Body of Worshippers, where people look at us and say, "Wow! Look at those people! They have to be followers of Christ! The proof is in the pudding! They worship God day in and day out, with every ounce of their being no matter what happens and no matter the cost!" Surely we know that, right? Well, you'd think so, but we have some problems. Why? Because if you look at most Churches it doesn't look like we're Worshipping the One and Only God. Are you kidding? It looks like we're worshipping anything and everything but God!

So, why in the world do we do this? Why do we Christians who are supposed to be worshippers of God, actually look like we've stopped worshipping God? Hey, great question. I'm glad you asked. It's pretty simple. The **first reason** why we've stopped worshipping God is because **We've Started Worshipping Our Things**.

Romans 1:21,24-25 "For although they knew God, they neither glorified him as God nor gave thanks to him, but their thinking became futile and their foolish hearts were darkened. Therefore God gave them over in the sinful desires of their hearts to sexual impurity for the degrading of their bodies with one another. They exchanged the truth of God for a lie, and worshiped and served created things rather than the Creator – who is forever praised. Amen."

Now folks, according to our text, the Bible is clear. One of the reasons why mankind has such foolish and darkened hearts is because of what? They refuse to glorify or worship God, right? And what was the evidence of it? They made a deliberate choice to worship created things instead of the Creator. Therefore, what did God do? He gave them over to their sinful desires and things got worse and worse from there on out, right?

People, the point is this. Surely the American Church knows this, right? I mean, surely we know that a true worshipper of Jesus Christ is never going to fall for the trap of worshipping created things instead of our Creator, right? I mean, surely we know if we do that our lives will get worse and worse, right? People, are you kidding? Let's be honest! We don't worship the One and Only God Who has made everything! We worship everything the One and Only God has made! Why? Because we've been tricked and seduced just like the Romans to worship created things instead of our Creator!

People, correct me if I'm wrong, but are we not told day in and day out that life is about getting a good job to get enough money to buy things we don't need to impress people we don't know who in the end are people who don't even care? Isn't that what they say life is all about? Does not our whole American Economy depend upon you and me becoming unrestrained consumers of things? Stop and think about it! Yeah, it might be real good for the American economy, but I'm here to tell you folks it's nothing more than old-fashioned idolatry! For those of you who don't believe me, let's get reacquainted with the definition of idolatry:

"D. Martin Lloyd-Jones states, 'A man's god is that for which he lives, for which he is prepared to give his time, his energy, his money, that which stimulates, rouses, excites, and enthuses him.'"[2]

Now folks, I'd say if we're spending the majority of our time chasing after things instead the Creator of things, then by that definition alone, those things have just become what? An idol, right? People, hello, idolatry is not only sinful, it's detrimental. There's a heavy price to pay! Why? Because stop and think about it! It takes a lot of what? It takes a lot of time to commit idolatry and to buy these things that nobody needs to impress people who don't even care. Therefore, your relationship with God, gets the short end if the stick! That's right! For those of you who still don't believe me that we actually do this to God, let's see just how much time we actually give to God:

If we live 75 years, this is how we would spend it...

Activity	Percentage of your time
23 years sleeping	31%
19 years working	25%
9 years watching TV or other amusements	12%
7.5 years in dressing and personal care	10%
6 years eating	8%
6 years traveling	8%
.5 year worshipping and praying	.07%[3]

Now folks, I'd say God's getting the short end of the stick here, you know what I'm saying? I mean, gee whiz, if He's that low of a priority in life, then maybe it's because there's an idol in our life. Therefore, the point is this. If we're guilty of spending more time with things instead of God, how in the world can we call ourselves worshippers of God? I mean, do we really think God doesn't notice?

Oh, but that's not all. The **second reason** why we've stopped worshipping God is because **We've Started Worshipping Our Titillation**.

Luke 4:1-8 "Jesus, full of the Holy Spirit, returned from the Jordan and was led by the Spirit in the desert, where for forty days he was tempted by the devil. He ate nothing during those days, and at the end of them he was hungry. The devil said to him, If you are the Son of God, tell this stone to become bread. Jesus answered, It is written: Man does not live on bread alone. The devil led him up to a high place and showed him in an instant all the kingdoms of the world. And he said to him, I will give you all their authority and splendor, for it has been given to me, and I can give it to anyone I want to. So if you worship me, it will all be yours. Jesus answered, It is written: Worship the Lord your God and serve him only."

Now folks, according to our text, the Bible is clear. The devil's ultimate goal in tempting Jesus wasn't just getting him to sin. It was to what? It was to get him to fall down and worship him, right? Here's my point. Notice what the devil used to try to get Jesus to do it. It wasn't just fame and fortune, it was what? It was about turning stones to bread, making yourself feel better, it was about personal satisfaction, right?

People, the point is this. Surely the American Church knows this, right? I mean, surely we know that a true worshipper of Jesus Christ is never going to fall for the trap of seeking personal satisfaction over the God of creation, right? People, are you kidding? Let's be honest! We don't get all excited over the God of Creation! We get all excited over entertaining titillation. Why? Because of idolatry! People, stop and think about it! Think about the devolving process with the Romans. Once they headed down the road of idolatry, what happened? Things got worse and worse, right? People, I'm telling you it's the same thing today. Once you start worshipping created things instead of the Creator, it not only consumes your time, it consumes your energy.

For instance, by the end of the week when we've run ourselves completely ragged in the rat race of idolatry, I mean consumerism, just so we can buy these things nobody needs in order to give them to people who already have everything, we're what? We're emotionally and physically wiped out, right? Here's the point! Instead of spending what time we have left with God to stay spiritually strong, what do we do? We spend it entertaining ourselves all weekend long. We don't seek a recharge from the God of Salvation. No! We seek a recharge in cable television! And we wonder why things get worse and worse! Do you see the devolving process? That's right! For those of you who still don't think we live like this, let's just see how much energy we give to entertainment over God:

1. The average household combined watches almost seven hours a day of television.

2. On the average, a child spends 1,680 minutes a week watching television. Compare that with the 38.5 minutes a week that he or she talks one-on-one with a parent.

3. By the time they reach kindergarten, the average American child has seen between 6,000 and 8,000 hours of television—approximately one-third of their total pre-school waking hours.

4. At maturity, they will have spent more time in front of a television than in any classroom.

5. By the age of ten, most children can name more brands of beer than Presidents.

6. The average American child or teenager views 10,000 murders, rapes, and aggravated assaults per year on television.

7. Children born today will witness 200,000 acts of violence on television by the time they are eighteen.

8. By the time today's children reach age seventy, they will have spent seven to ten years of their lives watching television.

9. Americans spend over 100 billion hours and over 100 billion dollars on legal forms of entertainment each year.

10. And don't forget...every package from hell comes disguised in ecstasy.[4]

Now folks, I'd say God's getting the short end of the stick again, you know what I'm saying? People living for titillation is not only another form of idolatry, it's one of satan's greatest trickeries, like this story reveals:

"One day the devil called a worldwide convention of his evil demons and said this, 'We can't keep the Christians from going to heaven, but we can keep them from forming an intimate relationship in Christ. If they gain that connection with Jesus, our power over them is broken. So, here's what we do.

Let's steal their time, so they can't gain any strength in Jesus Christ. Let's distract them by keeping them busy in the nonessentials of life and invent unnumbered schemes to occupy their minds. We'll over-stimulate their minds so that they cannot hear that still small voice.

We'll entice them to play the radio or cassette player whenever they drive; to keep the TV, the VCR, and their CD's going constantly in their homes. And we'll see to it that every store and restaurant in the world plays music constantly jamming their minds to break that union with Christ.

We'll fill their coffee tables with magazines and newspapers and pound their minds with the news twenty-four hours a day. We'll invade their driving moments with billboards and flood their mailboxes with junk mail, sweepstakes, mail order catalogues and every kind of newsletter and promotional offering promising false hopes.

We'll even get them to be excessive in their entertainment or recreation and send them to amusement parks, sporting events, concerts, and movies so they'll return exhausted, disquieted and unprepared for the coming week.

Even when they meet for spiritual fellowship, we'll involve them in gossip and small talk so that they leave with troubled consciences and unsettled emotion. Why, we'll crowd their lives with so many things that they have no time or energy to seek power from Christ.

It was quite a convention in the end. The demons went away eagerly causing Christians everywhere to get busy, busy, busy and rush here and there. Has the devil been successful at his scheme? You be the judge."[5]

Now folks, I'd say somebody's doing a great job of distracting us from what's really important in life, how about you? Gee whiz folks, could this be one of the reasons why we're so stinkin' spiritually dry, week after week? I mean, could it really be something as simple as we're entertaining ourselves to death? Makes you wonder, doesn't it? Not only that, the bigger point is this. If we spend more time with titillation instead of God, how in the world can we really call ourselves worshippers of God? I mean, do we really think He doesn't notice?

Oh, but that's not all. The **third reason** why we've stopped worshipping God is because **We've Started Worshipping Our Treasure**.

Matthew 6:24 "No one can serve two masters. Either he will hate the one and love the other, or he will be devoted to the one and despise the other. You cannot serve both God and Money."

Now folks, according to our text, the Bible is clear. Just like oil and water or chicken and cow, there's just some things in life that do not mix, you know what I'm saying? Folks, that's exactly what Jesus is saying here. He said you cannot mix or serve both God and what? Money, right? Why? Because one of them will ultimately become your master, right?

People, the point is this. Surely the American Church knows this, right? I mean, surely we know that a true worshipper of Jesus Christ is never going to fall for the trap of worshipping gold above God, right? People, are you kidding? Let's be honest! We don't like sharing our treasure for the kingdom of God! We like spending our treasure on the things of man! Just ask these guys:

"One day a $20 dollar bill ran into a $1 dollar bill on the conveyor belt at the Federal Reserve Building. As they were lying there side by side the $1 dollar bill said to the $20 dollar bill, 'Hey, mannnnnn, where have you

been. I haven't seen you in a long time?'

The $20 dollar bill replied, 'Man I've been having a ball! I've been traveling to distant countries, going to the finest restaurants and seeing tons of movies. In fact, I've been to Europe, a professional NBA game, Rodeo Drive, and I've just returned from all-day retreat spa. Man, I've done it all!'

So the $20 dollar bill asked the $1 dollar bill, 'So what about you? Where have you been.'

The $1 dollar bill said, 'Oh, you know, same old stuff, church, church, church.'

The $20 dollar bill replied, 'Uh, what's a Church?'"[6]

Now folks, that joke would be funny if it weren't so true, right? The point is this. Why is it true? Because of idolatry! That's right! Remember the devolving process? Worshipping created things instead of your Creator not only consumes your time and energy, it consumes your money. Why? Because stop and think about it! It takes a lot of money to buy these things that nobody needs in order to give them to people who already have everything, right? Therefore, God gets the short end of the stick again, right?

People, please don't misunderstand me. God doesn't want your money, He wants your heart. But one of the ways we find out if money has become our master is whether or not we'll use our money for the needs of the Master, like this guy did:

"One day a Christian doctor was asked by a patient what he'd done during the past week and this was his reply.

'On Monday I preached the gospel in Brazil. Tuesday I ministered among the Mexicans in southwest Texas. On Wednesday I operated on patients in a hospital in Africa. Thursday, I taught in a mission school in Japan. On

Friday I helped to establish a new Church in California. On Saturday, I taught classes in our seminaries and finally on Sunday I distributed Bibles in Korea.'

The astonished patient replied, "Well, how in the world can you be in so many places, doing so many different things?'

The doctor replied, 'I wasn't. But you see I hold the dollars God enabled me to earn and some of them have been channeled into the places of need I just mentioned.'"[7]

Now folks, I'd say that doctor was doing a pretty good job of using his money for God, how about you? Because of that, I'd say it was proof that money had not become his God, right? Therefore, the point is this. If we spend more time storing up treasure on earth instead of treasure in heaven, how in the world can we really call ourselves worshippers of the God of heaven? I mean, do we really think He doesn't notice?

You might be thinking, "Hey wait a minute. Here you go again. You're being too harsh! I mean, yeah okay, so maybe I haven't been giving God a whole lot of my time or my energy or even my money. But, so what? That's my decision! It only affects me!" Oh really? Well, I tell you what. I want you to read the following true story and you tell me if the way we worship God doesn't affect other people as well! This man shares what he had to encounter one time while ministering to the orphaned children in Haiti:

"We put an extension on to the school and the orphanage a few years ago to handle extreme cases. We were going to bring in a doctor with vitamin pills with extra food and we were going to take these kids that belonged to nobody and gather them up.

They slept in doorways on the verge of death and probably would be dead in five or six months if they didn't receive instant and immediate care. So we were going to gather them up and bring them to this extension on the orphanage that we had built and care for them and nurse them back to health.

The day came for us to pick them up and I went with my associate in a bus and drove up to the place where these children were to be assembled. We thought there were about fifty in the community. But, when we got there, there were three hundred of these kids.

Three hundred kids that belonged to nobody with their swelled stomachs, their emaciated bodies, and their black hair having turned rust color from malnutrition. Three hundred of them. We had room for fifty.

You know what I had to do. You know what I had to do. I had to stand there people, and out of that three hundred, I had to pick fifty to live. And you can't pick fifty to live without simultaneously choosing two hundred and fifty to die.

I did what I had to do and we loaded those fifty kids on that bus. I stayed behind with the other two hundred and fifty and I tried to cheer them up and tried to talk to them and tried to get them to sing some songs. And foolishly I got them to sing this gospel song. I didn't realize what I was getting them to sing!

They were singing before I realized it that little gospel chorus, 'God is so good, God is so good, God is so good to me.' And I went into the second stanza, 'He loves me so...' these dying kids with their swelled stomachs, with their falling out hair and with their emaciated bodies singing, 'He loves me so, He loves me so, God is so good to me.'

As they were singing that, something inside of me screamed against God and I was saying to my self, 'God, you're not good! God you don't care or else this wouldn't be happening!' And as sure as I am here, I sensed God speak to me in the depths of my being and say, 'I am good. And I do care. And you know why this is happening.' And I had to admit that I did know why it was happening.

God in His care and in His love has given to the Church the resources to respond to the needs of the world. And if the world is in need and if in fact the Church is not responding to those needs then it is only because the Church of Jesus Christ is not as faithful as it should be. Were doing a lot but were not doing near what we should do because God has called us to be that instrument that responds to the needs of the poor and the oppressed."

Now folks, I'd say there's a deadly price to pay when we refuse to worship God with all our heart, and soul and mind, how about you? People, keep in mind, that's just one scenario. Can you imagine how many millions of other people have already died and will keep on dying because the American Church keeps on refusing to worship God?

People, if we can't stop playing Church instead of being the Church then maybe it's time to get out of the Church. Why? Because being a Christian is not a game. What we say and do literally affects the eternal destiny of people around us. Therefore, it's high time we get rid of our practical amnesia. We have to remember who we are! We're not a bunch of heartless greedy idolaters of man. Are you kidding? We're a bunch of compassionate lovers of God! We're His Body. A **Body of Worshippers**!

Chapter Thirteen

A Body of Warriors

"One Sunday morning an old cowboy entered a Church service wearing grubby ol' jeans, a denim shirt, scuffed up boots and was carrying a worn out bible. However, the people of the congregation were all dressed with expensive clothes and accessories.

So, as the cowboy took a seat, the others not only moved away from him, but neither would they greet or even speak to him during the whole service. When the service was over and the old cowboy was leaving, a deacon approached him and asked the cowboy to do him a favor.

He said, 'Before you come back in here again, why don't you have a talk with God and ask Him what He thinks would be appropriate attire for coming here to worship.'

So, the old cowboy assured the deacon that he would. But sure enough, the next Sunday when he showed up for the services again, he was wearing the same ol' ragged clothes and was once again completely shunned and ignored.

Sure enough, the deacon approached him again and said, 'I thought I told you to speak to God about what you should wear before you came back to our Church services.' The old cowboy replied, 'Well, I did.'

The deacon said, 'Well, if you spoke to God, what did He tell you was the proper attire for worshiping in here?'

The cowboy said, 'Well, sir, God told me that He didn't have a clue what I should wear. He said He's never been here before!'"[1]

Now, how many of you guys have ever been to one of those kind of Church services? Sometimes you really do wonder if God's there, right? But folks, believe it or not, do you know wondering if God's really there is not only true for that one congregation? Do you know it's being repeated every single day across our whole nation? Hey, that's right! It really is. How? By Christians walking around acting like they have practical amnesia! Talk about God being absent!

Oh, we say we know who we are as the Church, but half the time, with our lips and with our lives, we act like we've forgotten who we are. It's not only detrimental in our walk with Christ. It keeps others from believing in Christ. Therefore, to avoid this atrocity of Christians living like they have practical amnesia by not knowing who they are, we're going to continue our study from the Word of God on the people of God entitled, **"The Character of the Church."**

We've already seen the first thing we need to know about the Church if we're going to stop acting like we have practical amnesia is that the Church is the Body of Christ. The second thing is that the Church is a Body of Brides. The third thing is that the Church is a Body of One. The fourth thing is that the Church is a Body of Hope. The fifth thing is that the Church is a Body of Joy. The sixth thing is that the Church is a Body of Love. The seventh thing is that the Church is a Body of Peace. The eighth thing is that the Church is a Body of Strangers. The ninth thing is that the Church is a Body of Disciples. The tenth thing is that the Church is a Body of Servants. The eleventh thing is that the Church is a Body of Rebels. In the last chapter we saw the twelfth thing we need to know is that the Church is a Body of Worshippers. There we saw that even though the Bible says were supposed to be worshippers of God, what are we doing? The American Church is worshipping all right, we're worshipping anything and everything but God! Why? Because we've started worshipping our things, we've started worshipping our titillation, and we've even started worshipping our treasure. Because of that, we're not only ceasing to be a Body of Worshippers, we're actually turning into a Body of heartless greedy idolaters of man. I don't think that's the kind of Church Jesus came to die for, how about you?

People, believe it or not, do you know that's not the only thing we need to know about the Church if we're going to stop acting like we have practical amnesia? The **thirteenth thing** we need to know is **The Church is a Body of Warriors**. But hey, don't take my word for it. Let's listen to God's:

2 Timothy 2:1-7 "You then, my son, be strong in the grace that is in Christ Jesus. And the things you have heard me say in the presence of many witnesses entrust to reliable men who will also be qualified to teach others. Endure hardship with us like a good soldier of Christ Jesus. No one serving as a soldier gets involved in civilian affairs – he wants to please his commanding officer. Similarly, if anyone competes as an athlete, he does not receive the victor's crown unless he competes according to the rules. The hardworking farmer should be the first to receive a share of the crops. Reflect on what I am saying, for the Lord will give you insight into all this."

Now folks, according to our text, the Bible is clear. The Apostle Paul encouraged Timothy to look at the Christian life in three different ways, didn't he? Notice what they were. He said to run like an athlete, work hard like a farmer, and fight like a what? Fight like a soldier or warrior, right! Not only that but just like a soldier we should what? We shouldn't get distracted with civilian life. We need to please who with our life? Our commanding officer. Can anybody guess Who that might be? Jesus!

Here's my point. Surely, we all know this, right? I mean, surely every Christian who has ever lived knows that the Church is to be a Body of Warriors who not only work hard, train hard, and fight hard to please their commanding officer, but they do so knowing we're in the midst of a great cosmic battle for the souls of men and women and there's no time to waste, right?" Well, you'd think so, but we have some problems. Why? Because if you look at most Churches it doesn't look like we're honing our skills becoming stronger warriors for God. Are you kidding? It looks like we're hiding in the hills trying to run from God!

So, why in the world do we do this? Why do we Christians who are supposed to be warriors of God fighting this great cosmic battle, actually look like we've stopped fighting the battle? Hey, great question. I'm glad you asked. It's pretty simple. The **first reason** why we've stopped fighting the great cosmic battle is because **We've Started Denying the Battle.**

Ephesians 6:10-12 "Finally, be strong in the Lord and in his mighty power. Put on the full armor of God so that you can take your stand against the devil's schemes. For our struggle is not against flesh and blood, but against the rulers, against the authorities, against the powers of this dark world and against the spiritual forces of evil in the heavenly realms."

Now folks, according to our text, the Bible is clear. One of the ways we Christians get strong in the Lord is by what? Is it by sleeping with the Bible under our pillow? Or is it by taping Gospel tracks to our eyelids? Or maybe it's putting an, "I love Jesus" bumper sticker on our car? No people! What did it say? It was by putting on the full armor of God, right? Why? Because what did Paul say? He said not all of our fights and struggles are natural, are they? No! What did he say? He said some of them are actually supernatural. Some of them actually come from the devil, right?

People, the point is this. Surely the American Church knows this, right? I mean, surely we know as true warriors of God that there's an actual demonic force out there whose sole purpose is to not only lead people to hell but to wreak havoc for Christians on their way to heaven, right? People, are you kidding? We are in trouble! We've been tricked and seduced by the devil. We're losing the battle and here's one of the reasons why. You see, everyone knows that if you want to win a war then one of the weapons you use is the element of surprise, the sneak attack, right? And what you do with a sneak attack is convince your enemy that you are nowhere to be found so that just when they relax their stance a little bit, you pounce on them and smash them before they even know what hit them.

So, here's the point. Surely we Christians would never fall for that ol' trick, would we? I mean, come on, didn't we just read that not all of our battles are against flesh and blood but some of them are from a demonic flood, right? People, are you kidding? The devil has us so bad that we are not only not fighting the great cosmic battle, but he actually has us denying that the battle exists in the first place! That's right! For those of you who don't believe me, let's look at what we Christians currently believe about the supernatural world:

1. 85% of all Americans identify themselves as Christians.

2. But 39% of Americans say that although Jesus Christ was crucified, He never had a physical resurrection. (Where do they get that from?)

3. Maybe it's from the 35% of Christians who say that although Jesus Christ was crucified, He never had a physical resurrection.

4. 54% of all Americans believe that if a person is generally good in life then they will earn a place in Heaven. (Where do they get that from?)

5. Maybe it's from the 38% of Christians who believe that if a person is good enough they can earn a place in Heaven.

6. Or maybe it's from the 11% of Christians who don't know what will happen when they die.

7. Or maybe it's from the 2% of Christians who believe that when they die they will not go to Heaven.

8. 69% of Americans don't believe that hell is an actual location of physical torment where people may be sent. (Where do they get that from?)

9. Maybe it's from the 65% of Christians who say that satan is "not a living being but is a symbol of evil." (Maybe this is why this Christian made this statement.)

10. "The Christian body in America is immersed in a crisis of Biblical illiteracy. How else can you describe matters when most Church-going adults reject the accuracy of the Bible, reject the existence of satan, claim that Jesus sinned, see no need to evangelize, and believe that good works are one of the keys to persuading God to forgive their sins. In many ways, we are living in an age of theological anarchy."[2]

Might I add, theological denial. People, I'd say the devil's sneak attack is working like a charm, how about you? In fact, I'd say he's doing a great job of getting us to deny the battle, how about you? Therefore, the point is this. If we can't stop denying the battle between the devil and God, how in the world can we call ourselves warriors of God? Hello! Do you see the obvious problem there?

Oh, but that's not all. The **second reason** why we've stopped fighting the great cosmic battle is because **We've Started Sabotaging the Battle**.

Galatians 5:13-15 "You, my brothers, were called to be free. But do not use your freedom to indulge the sinful nature; rather, serve one another in love. The entire law is summed up in a single command: Love your neighbor as yourself. If you keep on biting and devouring each other, watch out or you will be destroyed by each other."

Now folks, according to our text, the Bible is clear. Jesus Christ has set us free from sin, not so we can engage in sin, but what? So we can get busy serving and loving others because of Him, right? But that's not all. What was the second reason why we need to love each other? To protect us from devouring and destroying each other, right?

People, the point is this. Surely the American Church knows this, right? I mean, surely we know as true warriors of God that there's a serious danger in not loving each other as Christians because it could eventually lead to our downfall, right? People, are you kidding? We are in trouble! We've been tricked and seduced by the devil. We're losing the battle and here's another reason why. You see, everyone knows that if you want to win a war then one of the weapons you use is the element of antagonism. You let your enemy fight all right, but not against you, just against each other. And once they do, you can move in for the easy kill.

Here's the point. Surely we Christians would never fall for that ol' trick would we? I mean, surely we know if we spend all of our time fighting each other we'll never get around to fighting the enemy, right? People, are you kidding? The devil has us so bad that we're not only not fighting the great cosmic battle, but he actually has us sabotaging the battle! That's right! For those of you who don't believe me, let's listen to this quote from some former satanists and you tell me if the devil's not working hard to get us Christians to fight amongst ourselves:

"Christians are the satanists worst enemy. They are out to torment you. They are out to blackmail you. They will even kill you. They tried to kill me when I came out from black witchcraft."

"If you're in a Church where the Spirit of God is really moving and the Word of God is really being preached and where prayer is really going up to heaven for the salvation of souls, then they are going to regard you as their mortal enemy.

They will be out there trying everything they can to destroy, kill and to maim because that is of course the nature of satan and also the nature of his followers. They will try to infiltrate your Church. They will try to set up whispering campaigns against the Pastor and the elders. They may even try to seduce the Pastor."

"For two years I was involved in a Baptist Church. I was constantly complaining about the Pastor's sermons being too long, too dry, sowing discord among the people and gossiping about others."

"Some satanists who were handpicked, the most powerful ones, were sent into Church services to disrupt the meeting and we stopped people from going forward when they'd ask people to go forward and accept Christ as their Savior."

"I personally, in fact, was trained to learn all the Christian jargon. You know like, 'Hallelujah and praise the Lord' and say all the right things yet I had no idea of Jesus being my Savior than a man on the moon."

"If you can tear down the prayer foundation of a Church, then you've destroyed that Church. That's what every witch or satanist plans to do when they go into that Church. It's to tear down that prayer foundation. The rest of the Church goes quickly after that."[3]

Now folks, I'd say the devil's doing a pretty good job of getting us to fight against one another, how about you? Gee whiz, by the looks of all the Church problems, Church gossip and Church splits going on, I'd say it's not only causing satanic harm, it's working like a charm, how about you? Therefore, the point is this. If we can't stop sabotaging the battle between the devil and God, how in the world can we call ourselves warriors of God? Hello! Do you see the obvious problem here?

Oh, but that's not all. The **third reason** why we've stopped fighting the great cosmic battle is because **We've Started Running from the Battle**.

Jonah 1:1-3 "The word of the LORD came to Jonah son of Amittai: Go to the great city of Nineveh and preach against it, because its wickedness has come up before me. But Jonah ran away from the LORD and headed for Tarshish. He went down to Joppa, where he found a ship bound for that port. After paying the fare, he went aboard and sailed for Tarshish to flee from the LORD."

Now folks, according to our text, the Bible is clear. God specifically called Jonah to do what? To preach His truth against Nineveh the city of wickedness, right? Here's the point. What did Jonah do? Did he hop up lickety-split to go preach the truth over there? No! He wasted no time in high tailing it out of there, right? He simply refused to do what God called him to do!

People, the point is this. Surely the American Church knows this, right? I mean, surely we know as true warriors of God unlike Jonah, we jump at the chance to preach God's truth in a world full of wickedness and we'll face any heat or any persecution just for the cause of Christ, right? People, are you kidding? We are in trouble! We've been tricked and seduced by the devil. We're losing the battle and here's yet another reason why. You see, everyone knows that if you want to win a war then one of the weapons you use is the element of morale, right?

The first way you destroy your enemy's morale is by convincing them they're no longer qualified to fight so they'll give up on the fight, right? For instance, maybe you've heard some of the devils' lies before when you've blown it before. Maybe it sounded something like this, "Oh, you blew it now buddy! God won't forgive you for that one! Look at you! And you call yourself a warrior of God? Give me a break, you loser!" People, I'm here to tell you, once we buy into that lie, we'll not only stop fighting the great cosmic battle, but we'll actually get tricked into sitting down on the battlefield, never to get up again, like this story reveals:

"The Christian life is like standing at one end of a long, narrow street lined on both sides with two-story houses. At the other end of the street stands Jesus Christ, and as we walk towards Him we grow in maturity. There is absolutely nothing in the street which can keep me from reaching Jesus.

But since this world is influenced by satan, the row of houses on either side are inhabited by beings committed to keeping us from growing strong. So they hang out the windows and call to us,

'Hey, look over here! I've got something you really want!' or 'Hey, try this, there's nothing wrong with it. Or maybe it's this one, 'You're a worthless idiot and boy, you failed big this time. God can't use you now!'

Even though these voices have no real power to block our path, the strategy works all too well. You see, many Christians treat life's journey like a stroll through a shopping mall, instead of a race through a battlefield! Instead of staying focused on Christ, they give in to window-shopping at the enemy's stores!

The longer we linger, the easier it is for satan to keep us from running to Christ! The whole tactic is to simply get our eyes off of Jesus, slow down, sit down, stop, and if possible, give up on our journey with Jesus Christ."[4]

Now folks, I'd say the devil's doing a pretty good job of getting us to buy into his lies about God's forgiveness, how about you? Because of it, he's destroying our morale, is he not? People, my Bible says "greater is He that is in me than he that is in this world" and "if we confess our sins He is faithful and just to forgive us our sins and cleanse us from all unrighteousness." Therefore, stand up, rise up, and get up on the battlefield of life and start fighting again! Don't let him destroy your morale! Don't give into his lies! We're forever qualified to fight because we're forever forgiven by Christ!

Oh, but that's not all. The second way the enemy tries to destroy our morale is to convince us that we're no longer needed to fight. For instance, when the going gets tough and the battle's raging high, he simply tricks us to go run and hide! Maybe you've heard some of his lies, "You know, I'm getting way too old for this kind of thing. I think it's time to let the young whipper snappers to do God's work from now on." Or maybe it's "I'm getting sick and tired of all these headaches and conflicts and games people play. Let somebody else deal with it. I'm through!" Or maybe it's "I put in my time for the Lord. But now it's my time to go hide out in the hills and enjoy the rest of my life." How many of you heard that before?

People, stop and think about that logic? Can you imagine if George Washington was getting ready to cross the Delaware and he said, "You know, I'm just getting too old for this kind of thing. You young guys take care of this war. I'm out of here!" Or can you imagine on the beaches of Normandy if the soldiers cried out, "Hey, I'm sick of this conflict. I've got better things to do in life. I quit!" Or can you imagine if Jesus when He was hanging on the cross said, "All right, I've had it with you guys! I'm sick of your games! I'm going back to heaven and enjoy the rest of my life! You're on your own!" Can you imagine that?

Then people, where do we get off as Christians doing the very same thing? I mean, here we are in the midst of the greatest cosmic battle of all time, charged by God to save people from eternal destruction in hell, and we think we can just arbitrarily get up and run from the battle? That's not being a warrior of God? That's being a defector of God! But that's right! Don't take my word for it. Let's ask one of the greatest warriors of all time, Alexander the Great:

"Alexander the Great conquered the entire known world and part of his greatness was that he feared nothing at all. Therefore, the one thing he would not tolerate in any of his soldiers was cowardice.

One day when he was holding court for his army, the Sergeant at Arms brought in one soldier after another and read the accusations against them.

No eyes shifted and no one moved as the king pronounced sentence, often without mercy on one soldier after another. There was none who could deliver out of his hand and often the sentence was death.

Then suddenly came before him a soldier, a young man no more than about seventeen years of age. He was an unusual boy for that part of the world; blond, blue-eyed and handsome. For a moment the king looked at him in silence. No one moved. But they saw the hardness leave the king's face.

So Alexander the Great asked the Sergeant, 'What is his crime?' The sergeant replied, 'He was found fleeing the face of the enemy and was discovered cringing in a cave.' At that, the king's features hardened again, because the one thing he would not tolerate was cowardice.

But in the terrible silence that followed, as he looked on the boy, a remarkable thing happened. The king's face softened once more and he said, 'Son, what is your name?' And with those words, everyone in the hall knew that he had won the king's heart. So the boy breathed a sigh of relief and he answered, 'My name is Alexander.'

As soon as he said that the gentleness left the king's face and he said, 'What is your name?' The boy snapped to attention and replied, 'Alexander, Sir!'

And at that the king exploded out of his chair, grabbed the boy by his tunic, picked him up off his feet and said to him, 'Soldier, change your conduct or change your name!'"[5]

People of God, who do we think we're kidding? If we can't stop denying the battle, if we can't stop sabotaging the battle, and if we can't stop running from the battle, then what do we think we're acting like? We're not acting like a band of Christians. We're acting like a bunch of chickens! Therefore, I make the same charge to you today! Christian! Change your conduct, or change your name!

People, if we can't stop playing Church instead of being the Church then maybe it's time to get out of the Church. Why? Because being a Christian is not a game. What we say and do literally affects the eternal destiny of people around us. Therefore, it's high time we get rid of our practical amnesia. We have to remember who we are! We're not a bunch of namby-pamby-chicken-livered-Harvey-Milquetoast wimps. Are you kidding? We're the mighty brave army of the Almighty God! We're His Body. A **Body of Warriors**!

Chapter Fourteen

A Body of Witnesses

Hey, how many of you guys have stopped long enough in life to realize this truth. Do you know that each one of us is somebody else's weirdo? Have you ever thought about that? Hey, it's weird but it's probably true, you know? But that's right, for those of you who don't think of these kind of weird things in life like I do, I'm here to help you out. Let's take a look at several weird but true things I've thought about in life and let's see if you can agree.

- Is it true that marriage is a relationship in which one person is always right and the other is a husband?

- Is it true that on the sixth day, God created the platypus and God said, "Let's see the evolutionists try and figure this one out."

- Is it true that if Cher were to get cloned she would be Cher and Cher alike?

- Why is it that people keep running over a string a dozen times with their vacuum cleaner, then reach down, pick it up, examine it, then put it down to give their vacuum one more chance?

- Why is there Braille lettering on the Drive Thru ATM machines?

- If vegetarians love animals so much, why do they eat all their food?

- If at first you don't succeed, shouldn't you try doing it like your wife told you in the first place?

- If a man is standing in the middle of the forest speaking and there is no woman around, is he still wrong?

- Is it true that the number of people watching you is directly proportionate to the stupidity of your action?

- Why is it when you apply deodorant, you have to use the exact same number of swipes under each arm?

- Why is it that no one will answer the phone on the first ring? Why do you have to wait until the second ring?

- Why did our country remove the Ten Commandments from our courthouses yet we still make people swear to tell the whole truth and nothing but the truth on the Bible?[1]

Yes, there's lot's of weird but true things in life, aren't there? But folks, believe it or not, do you know I've discovered what has to be the all time weirdest but true thing in life that puts all those other ones to shame. Can anybody guess what that might be? Hey, that's right! It's Christians walking around acting like they have practical amnesia! Talk about weird but unfortunately true, right?

Oh, we say we know who we are as the Church, but half the time, with our lips and with our lives, we act like we've forgotten who we are. It's not only detrimental in our walk with Christ. It keeps others from believing in Christ. Therefore, to avoid this atrocity of Christians living like they have practical amnesia by not knowing who they are, we're going to continue our study from the Word of God on the people of God entitled, **"The Character of the Church."**

We've already seen the first thing we need to know about the Church if we're going to stop acting like we have practical amnesia is that the Church is the Body of Christ. The second thing is that the Church is a Body of Brides. The third thing is that the Church is a Body of One. The fourth thing is that the Church is a Body of Hope. The fifth thing is that the Church is a Body of Joy. The sixth thing is that the Church is a Body of Love. The seventh thing is that the Church is a Body of Peace. The eighth thing is that the Church is a Body of Strangers. The ninth thing is that the Church is a Body of Disciples. The tenth thing is that the Church is a Body of Servants. The eleventh thing is that the Church is a Body of Rebels. The twelfth thing is that the Church is a Body of Worshippers. In the last chapter we saw the thirteenth thing we need to know is that the Church is a Body of Warriors. There we saw that even though the Bible says were supposed to be warriors of God fighting the great cosmic battle, what are we doing? We've actually stopped fighting the great cosmic battle! Why? Because we've started denying the battle, we've started sabotaging the battle, and we've even started running from the battle. Because of that, we're not only ceasing to be a Body of Warriors, we're actually turning into a Body of namby-pamby-chicken-livered-Harvey-milquetoast wimps. I don't think that's the kind of Church Jesus came to die for, how about you?

People, believe it or not, do you know that's not the only thing we need to know about the Church if we're going to stop acting like we have practical amnesia? The **fourteenth thing** we need to know is **The Church is a Body of Witnesses**. But hey, don't take my word for it. Let's listen to God's:

Acts 1:1-8 "In my former book, Theophilus, I wrote about all that Jesus began to do and to teach until the day he was taken up to heaven, after giving instructions through the Holy Spirit to the apostles he had chosen. After his suffering, he showed himself to these men and gave many convincing proofs that he was alive. He appeared to them over a period of forty days and spoke about the kingdom of God. On one occasion, while he was eating with them, he gave them this command: Do not leave Jerusalem, but wait for the gift my Father promised, which you have heard me speak about. For John baptized with water, but in a few days you will be baptized with the Holy Spirit. So when they met together, they asked him, Lord, are you at this time going to restore the kingdom to Israel? He said to them: It is not for you to know the times or dates the Father has set by his own authority. But you will receive power when the Holy Spirit comes on you; and you will be my witnesses in Jerusalem, and in all Judea and Samaria, and to the ends of the earth."

Now folks, according to our text, the Bible is clear. One of the reasons why God gives us His Spirit at salvation is for the power to what? Was it the power to get wild and crazy or the power to wow people with our spiritual abilities or maybe the power to lift heavy weights for Jesus? No people! What did it say? God gives us His powerful spirit so we can be what? Powerful witnesses, right? But that's not all. Notice what else Jesus said. He didn't say we might be His powerful witnesses. He didn't say we need to think about being powerful witnesses, what did He say? He said you will be my witnesses, right?

Here's my point. Surely, we all know this, right? I mean, surely every Christian who has ever lived knows that the Church is to be a Body of Witnesses, who not only witness to others because Jesus commanded it but we even do so across the face of our planet, to the ends of the earth, right? Well, you'd think so, but we have some problems. Why? Because if you look at most Churches it doesn't look like we're willing witnesses declaring the gospel of God. Are you kidding? It looks like we're disobedient Christians ashamed of God!

So, why in the world do we do this? Why do we Christians who are supposed to be witnesses for Christ declaring the gospel to the lost, actually look like we've stopped witnessing to the lost? Hey, great question. I'm glad you asked. It's pretty simple. The **first reason** why we've stopped witnessing to the lost is because **We've Stopped Praying for the Lost**.

Romans 10:1-4 "Dear brothers and sisters, the longing of my heart and my prayer to God is that the Jewish people might be saved. I know what enthusiasm they have for God, but it is misdirected zeal. For they don't understand God's way of making people right with himself. Instead, they are clinging to their own way of getting right with God by trying to keep the law. They won't go along with God's way. For Christ has accomplished the whole purpose of the law. All who believe in him are made right with God."

Now folks, according to our text, the Bible is clear. One of the Apostle Paul's greatest longings in life was what? He longed that the Jewish people might be saved, right? Why? Because they were going the wrong way instead of God's way to get to heaven, right? They were trying to get to heaven some other way than through Jesus, right? People don't do that today, do they? Yeah, right! Not only that. Notice what else Paul said. He didn't just long for their salvation, he what? He earnestly prayed for their salvation, right? He went to God on their behalf.

People, the point is this. Surely the American Church knows this, right? I mean, surely we know as witnesses of Christ that if we really love somebody we'll not only long for them to be saved, but we'll be sucking carpet day in and day out praying to God they do get saved, right? People, are you kidding? We're not praying to God on behalf of the lost. We're praying for anything and everything but the lost. We pray for healing, we pray for health. We pray for jobs and we pray for wealth. For some goofy reason, we hardly spend any time praying for the lost. People, please don't misunderstand me. It's not that we can't pray for those other things as well. Hello! It's just for some goofy reason, the most important thing to pray for in life has become the least thing we pray for in life. Therefore, to remind us what's really important in life, let's see what we need to be praying for:

1. If we pray for someone to be healed of cancer but they still don't know Christ, what good is that?

2. If we pray that our kids do well in school but they don't know the Savior, what good is that?

3. If we pray that our loved ones find a good job but they still don't have a relationship with God, what good is that?

4. If we pray for someone's practical needs, yet getting saved, their greatest spiritual need isn't met, what good is that?

5. If we pray for someone to get a house yet they're not going to a mansion in heaven, what good is that?

6. If we pray for God to fix a person's car but not to fix their soul, what good is that?

7. If we pray for a loved one's financial need but they still don't have eternal riches in Christ, what good is that?

8. If we pray for somebody having heart surgery yet they haven't been given a new heart from Jesus, what good is that?

9. If we pray for someone in a depressing situation yet they still don't know the joy of salvation, what good is that?

10. If we pray for someone to have traveling mercies but they're still traveling to hell, what good is that?[2]

Now folks, I'd say the most important thing in life to pray for really is the least thing we pray for, isn't it? In fact, I'd say we've plum forgotten what life is all about, like this story reveals:

"Years ago when the first Church Buildings were built in America, the graveyard was not only built within the Churchyard, but the Church buildings themselves had clear windows instead of stained glass. Why?

Because they wanted the Pastor to see the graveyard while he preached so he'd be reminded of the urgency of his message! Every time he looked out a window he was constantly reminded that everybody who sat in the pews right before him, as he spoke, would eventually fill a place in that cemetery outside that window and ultimately have to stand before God to be judged.

You see, back then, the first and foremost priority of the Church in America, was to bring men and women into a right relationship with the Lord Jesus Christ.

But now our Church Sanctuaries are built with windows you can't see through and a cemetery nowhere to be found. Because of that, we've not only forgotten what life is all about, but we no longer see the real work that needs to be done!"[3]

Now folks, I'd say if we're no longer praying for the lost, then something is simply clouding our view of eternity, isn't it? We've forgotten what life's all about, haven't we? Not only that, the point is this. If we've actually stopped praying for the lost who still don't know Jesus Christ, how can we call ourselves true witnesses of Christ? Hello! Do you see the obvious problem there?

Oh, but that's not all. The **second reason** why we've stopped being witnesses to the lost is because **We've Stopped Sharing with the Lost**.

Romans 1:14-16 "I am obligated both to Greeks and non-Greeks, both to the wise and the foolish. That is why I am so eager to preach the gospel also to you who are at Rome. I am not ashamed of the gospel, because it is the power of God for the salvation of everyone who believes: first for the Jew, then for the Gentile."

Now folks, according to our text, the Bible is clear. Another one of the Apostle Paul's greatest longings in life was what? It wasn't just to pray for the lost, it was to what? It was to share the gospel with the lost, right? Why? Because what did he say? He said the gospel has the power of God to save anyone, Jew or Gentile, who believes in it, right? Therefore, Paul was not what? He was not ashamed of the gospel, right?

People, the point is this. Surely the American Church knows this, right? I mean, surely we know as witnesses of Christ that there's no stinkin' reason to be ashamed of the gospel. I mean, gee whiz, what's there to be ashamed about showing others how to get to heaven, right? People, are you kidding? We're not only not praying for the lost but neither are we sharing the gospel with the lost. We're actually acting like we're ashamed of the gospel.

For instance, maybe you've heard comments like these, "Well, what if they reject me?" or "What if they think I'm weird?" or "I don't want them to think I'm judging them." or "What if they get all mad at me and don't want to be my friend anymore?" Have you heard those comments before? People, stop and think about it. Isn't that implying the gospel is bad? Isn't that assuming it's something to be ashamed of? People, here's what's so ironic. I mean, here we have the gospel, which means good news and yet we're treating it like it's the what? The bad news! To show you how crazy this behavior is, let's look at this same kind of behavior in a different scenario:

1. Can you imagine if a lifeguard refused to save a drowning person?

2. Can you imagine if a paramedic refused to perform CPR?

3. Can you imagine if a heart surgeon refused to do heart surgery on a patient?

4. Can you imagine if a doctor refused to tell a cancer patient that they have cancer and unless they get treatment they will die?

5. Can you imagine if a policeman refused to protect you from a burglar?

6. Can you imagine if a S.W.A.T. team member refused to rescue a hostage?

7. Can you imagine if a person took a lifeboat from a sinking ship and refused to let anyone else in?

8. Can you imagine if a parent refused to rescue their child from getting hit by a car?

9. Can you imagine if a fireman refused to rescue someone from a fire?

10. Then why is it acceptable for a Christian not to witness to the lost who are in danger of the fires of hell?[4]

Now folks, I'd say when you put it into its context, a Christian refusing to share the gospel is one of the most unimaginable behaviors of all time, how about you? Not only that, the point is this. If we've actually stopped sharing the gospel to the lost who don't know Jesus Christ, how can we call ourselves true witnesses of Christ? Hello! Do you see the obvious problem there?

Oh, but that's not all. The **third reason** why we've stopped being witnesses to the lost is because **We've Stopped Caring for the Lost**.

Luke 16:22-28 "The time came when the beggar died and the angels carried him to Abraham's side. The rich man also died and was buried. In hell, where he was in torment, he looked up and saw Abraham far away, with Lazarus by his side. So he called to him, Father Abraham, have pity on me and send Lazarus to dip the tip of his finger in water and cool my tongue, because I am in agony in this fire. But Abraham replied, Son, remember that in your lifetime you received your good things, while Lazarus received bad things, but now he is comforted here and you are in agony. And besides all this, between us and you a great chasm has been fixed, so that those who want to go from here to you cannot, nor can anyone cross over from there to us. He answered, Then I beg you, father, send Lazarus to my father's house, for I have five brothers. Let him warn them, so that they will not also come to this place of torment."

Now folks, according to our text, the Bible is clear. The reason why we as Christians share the gospel is not only because it's the way to go to heaven, it's what? It's the way we get to escape from going to hell, right? How many of you guys would say the ol' rich man there was having a great time where he was at? No, it was pretty horrible, wasn't it?

People, the point is this. Surely the American Church knows this, right? I mean, surely we know as witnesses of Christ that if we really love somebody we'll do whatever it takes to share the gospel and we'll certainly never give up in sharing the gospel because we care way too much to see others end up in a place like that, right? People, are you kidding? We're not caring for the lost doing whatever it takes to save every last man, woman and child. We care only for our own lives living it up and partying wild. Why? Because frankly folks, we don't want to deal with reality. We don't want to hear, we don't want to listen, and we certainly don't want to be confronted with the reality of hell. Are you kidding? Why, it's become the deadly "H" word in the American Church. People, what's goofy is we can deny it all we want but hell exists whether we like it or believe it or not! Hello! I didn't say that, Jesus did!

People this is precisely why Jesus talked more about hell than He ever did about heaven. He didn't do it out of fear or hate! Are you kidding? He did it out of love! Why? Because people, hell is one place you don't ever want to go! But don't take my word for it, let's listen to God's. Let see what hell is like:

1. Place of Thirst: (Luke 16)
2. Place of Worms: (Mark 9)
3. Place of No Return: (Luke 16)
4. Place of Remembrance: (Luke 16)

5. Place of the Wicked Dead: (Luke 10)
6. Place of the Wicked Demons: (2 Peter 2)
7. Place of a Bottomless Pit: (Luke 8)
8. Place of a Burning Waste Dump: (Matt. 23)

9. Place of Outer Darkness: (Matt. 8)
10. Place of Fire: (Rev. 20)

11. Place of the Lake of Fire: (Rev. 20)
12. Place of Eternal Fire: (Matt. 18)

13. Place of Unquenchable Fire: (Mark 9)
14. Place of Everlasting Punishment: (Matt. 25)
15. Place of Eternal Condemnation: (Mark 3)
16. Place of Eternal Judgment: (Heb. 6)

17. Place of Everlasting Destruction: (2 Thess. 1)
18. Place of Weeping & Gnashing of Teeth: (Matt. 13)
19. Place of Torment: (Luke 16)
20. Place of Eternal Torment: (Rev. 20)[5]

Now folks, I'd say hell's not a very fun place to be, how about you? Gee whiz, no wonder Jesus talked about it so much. I mean if you really love somebody, you care enough to warn them about a place like that, right? You might be saying, "Well, wait a second. If I start telling people about hell, I might scare them off." Well folks, I like what one guy said. He said, "Well, hello! Where do you think you're going to scare them off too? Hell #2?" People, stop and think about it! If hell really exists, and it does, then don't you think people need to know about it? I mean, gee whiz, even an atheist can figure that one out, right? Well, for those of you who aren't sure, I have some proof. Let's listen to a testimony of two atheists who are confronted with the actual reality of hell and you tell me if even they can figure out what to do:

"Dr. Maurice Rawlings, a renown specialist in the field of internal medicine and cardiovascular disease, resuscitated many people who had been clinically dead. Some of whom experienced visions of the torments of hell. After the resuscitation of Charles McKay, both Dr. Rawlings and his patient McKay immediately turned their lives over to the Lord for salvation. Here is their testimony.

Dr Rawlings: 'The strangest thing happened when I would stop resuscitating to put in a pacemaker.'

Mr. McKay: 'When I came to, Dr. Rawlings said my hair was literally standing on the end and my eyes had already started to dilate. I was just absolutely scared to death. I was horrified. I parted lots.

What had led to this was earlier they sent me on up to the clinic where Dr. Rawlings was and kept me for about three or four days and then gave me a stress test. On the stress test, I told the girl, Pam, that was giving the stress test that I was dying, let me off. That was the last that I remember.

When I came to, Dr. Rawlings was giving me CPR. He asked me what was the matter because I was looking so scared. I told him I had been to hell and I need help. He said, 'Keep your hell to yourself. I'm a doctor and I'm trying to save your life. You need a Minister for that.'

As he was giving me CPR, he was trying to install a pacemaker with one hand and trying to continue CPR with the other. I would start to fade out and he would start CPR again and bring me back. I watched what was going on like I was floating in the air. I was up above and looked down and could see things.

I kept asking them, 'Please help me! Please help me! I don't want to go back to hell!' And Pam said, 'Well, he needs help. Do something!' And at that time Dr. Rawlings said, 'Pray this short prayer after me. I believe that Jesus Christ is the Son of God. If you save my soul and keep me alive, I'll be hooked to you forever. And if I die, please keep me out of hell.'

After I prayed that, all the other experiences were real pleasant. This light surrounded me and to this day I believe it was the Holy Spirit that took care of me. I never felt so good and so safe in all my life.'

Dr. Rawlings: 'After all this was over, I realized what had really happened. It was a double conversion. Not only had this make believe prayer converted this atheist on the floor, it had also converted this atheist doctor that was working on him. That's the only reason I can appear to you here now. It's to tell you that there is a life after death, and it ain't all good!'"[6]

Now folks, I find it awfully strange that when the rubber meets the road and you're staring hell right in the face, that even an atheist cares enough to share the gospel, how about you? Therefore, who do we think we're kidding. If we don't pray for the lost, if we don't share with the lost, and if we don't even care enough to warn the lost about hell, then what do we think we're acting like? We're not acting like witnesses of Christ. We're acting like we're ashamed of Christ! We're actually calling Jesus a liar!

People, if we can't stop playing Church instead of being the Church then maybe it's time to get out of the Church. Why? Because being a Christian is not a game. What we say and do literally affects the eternal destiny of people around us. Therefore, it's high time we get rid of our practical amnesia. We have to remember who we are! We're not a bunch of atheistic close-mouthed people ashamed of the gospel. Are you kidding? We're the mouthpieces of Christ lovingly proclaiming the gospel! We're His Body. A **Body of Witnesses!**

Chapter Fifteen

A Body of Winners

"During the 1950's, this so-called Pastor preached a social gospel of human freedom, equality, and love, and created a Church that was an *inter-racial mission for the sick, homeless and jobless. And before you knew it, this quasi-Pastor has assembled a large following of over 900 members.*

Everything seemed to be going fine until the government investigated his supposed cures for cancer, heart disease and arthritis. And after being under this scrutiny, they decided to move the group to Ukiah in Northern California and later to San Francisco and then to Los Angeles.

But it wasn't long before suspicions were being raised of illegal activities within the Church and so this supposed man of God moved some of the people to Guyana where they leased about 4,000 acres of dense jungle from the local government there.

And soon this self-proclaimed prophet developed a belief he called Translation in which he and his followers would all die together and would move to another planet for a life of bliss.

But soon, authorities from the United States came to check out the rumors that this place was being run like a concentration camp, and that people were being held there against their will.

So when they were getting ready to leave, the armed Church security guards opened fire and killed one U.S. congressman and four other people. And now fearing retribution, the leaders reached a consensus to commit group suicide.

And so when all was said and done, on November 18th, 1978, some 914 people had died: 638 adults and 276 children. The Church was called The People's Temple and the so-called Pastor was...Jim Jones."[1]

Now folks, with all due respect to the families involved, I'd say that supposed Pastor and that supposed Church left behind a horrible trail of death and destruction, how about you? But folks, believe it or not, do you know this same deadly scenario is being played out all across America every single day. And get this! It's not causing the destruction of just hundreds of lives, but millions of lives. Can anybody guess what that might be? Hey, that's right! It's the American Church walking around acting like they have practical amnesia! You talk about deadly behavior!

Oh, we say we know who we are as the Church, but half the time, with our lips and with our lives, we act like we've forgotten who we are. It's not only detrimental in our walk with Christ. It keeps others from believing in Christ. Therefore, to avoid this atrocity of Christians living like they have practical amnesia by not knowing who they are, we're going to conclude our study from the Word of God on the people of God entitled, **"The Character of the Church."**

We've already seen the first thing we need to know about the Church if we're going to stop acting like we have practical amnesia is that the Church is the Body of Christ. The second thing is that the Church is a Body of Brides. The third thing is that the Church is a Body of One. The fourth thing is that the Church is a Body of Hope. The fifth thing is that the Church is a Body of Joy. The sixth thing is that the Church is a Body of Love. The seventh thing is that the Church is a Body of Peace. The eighth thing is that the Church is a Body of Strangers. The ninth thing is that the Church is a Body of Disciples. The tenth thing is that the Church is a Body of Servants. The eleventh thing is that the Church is a Body of Rebels. The twelfth thing is that the Church is a Body of Worshippers. The thirteenth thing is that the Church is a Body of Warriors. In the last chapter we saw the fourteenth thing we need to know is that the Church is a Body of Witnesses. There we saw that even though the Bible says were supposed to be witnesses for Christ declaring the gospel to the lost, what are we doing? It looks like we've actually stopped witnessing to the lost! Why? Because we've stopped praying for the lost, we've stopped sharing with the lost, and because of that we've stopped caring for the lost. Because of that, we're not only ceasing to be a Body of Witnesses, we're actually turning into a Body of atheistic close-mouthed people ashamed of the gospel. I don't think that's the kind of Church Jesus came to die for, how about you?

People, believe it or not, do you know that's not the only thing we need to know about the Church if we're going to stop acting like we have practical amnesia? The **fifteenth thing** we need to know is **The Church is a Body of Winners**. But hey, don't take my word for it. Let's listen to God's:

John 16:17-33 "Some of his disciples said to one another, What does He mean by saying, In a little while you will see me no more, and then after a little while you will see me, and because I am going to the Father? They kept asking, What does He mean by a little while? We don't understand what He is saying. Jesus saw that they wanted to ask Him about this, so He said to them, Are you asking one another what I meant when I said, In a little while you will see me no more, and then after a little while you will see me? I tell you the truth, you will weep and mourn while the world rejoices. You will grieve, but your grief will turn to joy. A woman giving birth to a child has pain because her time has come; but when her baby is born she forgets the anguish because of her joy that a child is born into the world. So with you: Now is your time of grief, but I will see you again and you will rejoice, and no one will take away your joy. In that day you will no longer ask Me anything. I tell you the truth, My Father will give you whatever you ask in My Name. Until now you have not asked for anything in My name. Ask and you will receive, and your joy will be complete. Though I have been speaking figuratively, a time is coming when I will no longer use this kind of language but will tell you plainly about My Father. In that day you will ask in My Name. I am not saying that I will ask the Father on your behalf. No, the Father Himself loves you because you have loved Me and have believed that I came from God. I came from the Father and entered the world; now I am leaving the world and going back to the Father. Then Jesus' disciples said, Now You are speaking clearly and without figures of speech. Now we can see that You know all things and that You do not even need to have anyone ask you questions. This makes us believe that You came from God. You believe at last! Jesus answered. But a time is coming, and has come, when you will be scattered, each to his own home. You will leave Me all alone. Yet I am not alone, for my Father is with me. I have told you these things, so that in Me you may have peace. In this world you will have trouble. But take heart! I have overcome the world."

Now folks, according to our text, the Bible is clear. Jesus clearly told His disciples that they would have a temporary time of grief, speaking of course about His crucifixion, but when He rose from the grave, they would have a what? A permanent joy, right? In fact, it was a joy that no one can take away! Why? Because Jesus has overcome the world! He whooped the devil's pants off on the cross! He won! Therefore, since we belong to Him that makes us a bunch of what? Winners!

Surely we know that, right? I mean, surely we know that the Church is a Body of Winners because Jesus won the ultimate victory! He defeated sin, death and hell and since we belong to Him we're on the winning team! Therefore, we always have a victorious attitude and outlook on life, right? Well, you'd think so, but we have some problems. Why? Because if you look at most Churches it doesn't look like we're victorious winners in Christ. Are you kidding? By the looks on our faces and our attitudes in life, it looks like were a bunch of losers in Christ!

So, why in the world do we do this? Why do we Christians who are supposed to be a Body of victorious winners in Christ, actually look like a bunch of losers in Christ? Hey, great question. I'm glad you asked. It's pretty simple. The **first reason** why we look like a bunch of losers in Christ is because we've forgotten that Christ has won for us a **Forever Pardon of Sin**.

Romans 7:21-8:2 "So I find this law at work: When I want to do good, evil is right there with me. For in my inner being I delight in God's law; but I see another law at work in the members of my body, waging war against the law of my mind and making me a prisoner of the law of sin at work within my members. What a wretched man I am! Who will rescue me from this body of death? Thanks be to God – through Jesus Christ our Lord! So then, I myself in my mind am a slave to God's law, but in the sinful nature a slave to the law of sin. Therefore, there is now no condemnation for those who are in Christ Jesus, because through Christ Jesus the law of the Spirit of life set me free from the law of sin and death."

Now folks, according to our text, the Bible is clear. The Apostle Paul discovered a strange law at work in the Christian life, didn't he? What was that strange law? It was that we Christians not only sin before we get saved, but what? We sin after we get saved, right? How many of you can testify to that? Well, the rest of you just did by lying. But anyway, notice what else he said. He said even though we commit these acts of wretched sin, what does God do? Does He beat us over the head with a two-by-four? Does He tell us, "Get out of My face! I never want to see you again?" Or maybe does He threaten us with losing our salvation? No people! What did it say? We don't lose our salvation. Why? Because in Christ there is no condemnation, right? We're forever pardoned of all our sins.

People, the point is this. Surely the American Church knows this, right? I mean, surely we know we're winners in Christ because we have eternal forgiveness of sin. Therefore, no matter what happens in life, we always have a huge smile on our face, right? People, are you kidding? We don't look like a bunch of winners! We look like a bunch of losers! If you look at most Christians today, it looks like their diet consists of sour pickles, lemons, and prunes! Why? Because it's simple people! We have our eyes off of Christ. We've forgotten the victory we have in Him and instead only see ourselves still covered in sin!

People, this is what's so amazing about the gospel! God doesn't forgive us of just some of our sin. He forgives us of all our sin! In fact, so much so that right now, not tomorrow, not in the future, but right now God sees us as if we had never sinned. Therefore, to remind us of this amazing victory over sin we have in Jesus Christ, let's listen to this man's realization that our sins are "erased" and you tell me if we don't have something to celebrate in life as Christians:

"I always had this fear of going to heaven. You say, 'Afraid of going to heaven?' You bet! You say, 'I thought it was hell?' I wasn't afraid of hell. I mean, I figured if I went to hell at least they would accept me there. You know, they wouldn't say you're not good enough. But heaven, I had the feeling that they were going to pull down this movie screen and place this video tape of all the sins I've ever committed. And my mother would be there!

Now people, I don't know if they have a tape on me recording all my sins. And I don't know if they have a tape on you recording all your sins. But if there is such a tape, I've got good news for you. Jesus has erased your tape! Your sin says the Scripture is blotted out, it is buried in the deepest sea, it is remembered no more.

That thrills me, not just to have my sins forgiven, but forgotten. I don't know how you're going to heaven but I am going to move. You see, I am from West Philadelphia. In Philadelphia you don't walk. They'll kill you if you walk. You move man! You see, people back off when you move. That's how I'm going to walk into heaven. I'm going to move and I'm going to yell at the angels, 'Out of my way angels!' Well, they're only messengers.

And I'm going to strut before the Lord and Jesus will be there with all my sins forgiven, forgotten, buried in the deepest sea, remembered no more. Isn't that incredible? And with a record that is washed clean, with sins that are purged, the Father will embrace me and I can call Him Abba Father."

Now folks, I'd say we have lots to celebrate in life as Christians, how about you? I mean, gee whiz, you talk about an amazing victory, right? Therefore, the point is this. If we're walking around in life looking like a loser in Christ instead of a winner in Christ, could it be something as simple as we have our eyes off of Him and on to our sin? Could it be we've forgotten that Jesus has won for us a forever pardon of sin? I kind of think so!

Oh, but that's not all. The **second reason** why we look like a bunch of losers in Christ is because we've forgotten that Christ has won for us a **Fantastic Paradise with Him**.

Hebrews 11:24-26 "By faith Moses, when he had grown up, refused to be known as the son of Pharaoh's daughter. He chose to be mistreated along with the people of God rather than to enjoy the pleasures of sin for a short time. He regarded disgrace for the sake of Christ as of greater value than the treasures of Egypt, because he was looking ahead to his reward."

Now folks, according to our text, the Bible is clear. The great and mighty man of God, Moses, made a deliberate choice to do what? He chose to be mistreated with the people of God instead of enjoying the pleasure of sin, right? Why did he do that? Was it because he was looking forward to being blessed by God to get a brand new chariot with chrome wheels? Or maybe he was looking forward to getting elected on the Egyptian Church board? No people! What did it say? He didn't do it because He was wanting to get on a Church board. He did it for a what? For a heavenly reward, right?

People, the point is this. Surely the American Church knows this, right? I mean, surely we know just like Moses that we not only have a forever forgiveness of sin through the Messiah but we get to spend eternity in a fabulous paradise with the Messiah. Therefore, we can endure any problem or any trial on earth because we know we have something way better coming. We have something to look forward to, right? People, are you kidding? We don't look like a bunch of winners! We look like a bunch of losers! If you look at most Christians today, it looks like they just got audited by the IRS, somebody ran over their dog and their house just burnt down! Why? Because it's simple folks! Once again, we have our eyes off of Christ. We not only still see ourselves covered in sin. We've forgotten we get to spend eternity in a paradise with Him. People, this paradise or heaven is one place that will not only blow your mind, but it's a place where once for all you will leave all of your troubles, and I mean all of them, forever behind like these nurses found out:

"One day there were three nurses who died and went to Heaven and there they were met by Saint Peter who asked them. 'What did you used to do back on Earth and why should you be allowed into Heaven?'

So the first nurse told Peter, 'I was a nurse at an inner city hospital. I suffered long and worked hard to bring healing and peace to as many sufferers as possible, especially the poor children.'

So Saint Peter said, 'Very noble. You may enter.' And he ushered her through the gates.

So he turned to the next nurse and asked her the same question, 'What did you used to do back on Earth and why should you be allowed into Heaven?'

The second nurse replied, 'I was a missionary nurse in the Amazon. I suffered for many years and worked day and night with a small group of doctors and nurses to help people in numerous tribes, healing them and telling them of God's love.'

'Excellent!' said Saint Peter. And he ushered her through the gates as

well.

Well, finally he posed the same question to the third nurse. But she hesitated and then replied sheepishly, 'I was just a nurse at an HMO.'

So Saint Peter considered her answer for a moment and then told her, 'Well, okay. You can enter, too.'

The nurse exclaimed in relief. 'Wow! For a moment there, I almost thought you weren't going to let me in.'

To which Saint Peter replied, 'Oh, you can certainly come in, but you can only stay for three days.'"[2]

Now folks, I'm personally looking forward to not having to deal with any more HMO's, how about you? No wonder it's called heaven! Hello! People, let's not just take the word of those nurses. Let's take a look at some Bible verses. Let's see what the Bible says heaven is like:

1. The Dwelling Place of God: (Psalm 2)
2. The Dwelling Place of Angels: (Matt. 18)
3. A Heavenly Country: (Heb. 11)
4. A Holy Place: (Isaiah 57)

5. An Eternal Paradise: (1 Cor. 12)
6. A Place with Streets of Gold: (Rev. 21)
7. A Place with Gates of Pearls: (Rev. 21)
8. A Place with Foundations of Precious Gems: (Rev. 21)

9. A Place of Eternal Rest: (Rev. 14)
10. A Place of Eternal Joy: (Rev. 7)
11. A Place Without Wickedness: (Rev. 22)
12. A Place Without Darkness: (Rev. 21)

13. A Place Without Sin: (Rev. 21)
14. A Place Without Tears: (Rev. 21)

15. A Place Without Mourning: (Rev. 21)
16. A Place Without Pain: (Rev. 21)

17. A Place Without Death: (Rev. 21)
18. A Place of Absolute Purity: (Rev. 21)
19. A Place Filled with the Glory of God: (Rev. 21)
20. An Everlasting Place: (2 Cor. 5)[4]

Now folks, I'd say we Christians really do have a lot to look forward to, how about you? Oh, but that is still just the tip of the iceberg! This man stretches our minds even further about what heaven might be like:

"I taught Physics and I'll give you one of my little theories about what heaven might be like. The electromagnetic spectrum contains all the different wavelengths, like radio waves, microwaves, and including a small piece called light. Now your eyeball can see the colors, red, orange, yellow, green, blue, violet, that's all.

The spectrum goes forever in both directions beyond that. Suppose we get to heaven and God gives us new eyes that can see the entire spectrum. That means there will be brand news colors, trillions of them. Not new shades of our current colors...but brand new colors! That's why heaven has to be so large. It's for the women's closets!

But can you imagine if we get new eyes that can see the whole spectrum? You're going to be able to see the sounds coming off the piano. Right now we can only hear them. Imagine seeing the sounds. What if we get new ears that can hear the whole spectrum? You're going to be able to hear the colors, or smell them, or taste them!

We've only got five senses folks. Maybe there's more. But if God just took these five and expanded them to the max, we would spend forever walking around heaven going, "Wow! Did you smell that? Here, lick that! Wow!"[3]

Now folks, I'd say any trial and any heartache we ever face on this earth, is going to pale in comparison to the awesome reality of heaven, how about you? Therefore, the point is this. If we're walking around in life looking like a loser in Christ instead of a winner in Christ, could it be something as simple as we have our eyes off of heaven and on this earth? Could it be we've forgotten that Jesus has won for us a fantastic paradise with Him? I kind of think so!

Oh, but that's not all. The **third reason** why we look like a bunch of losers in Christ is because we've forgotten Christ has won for us a **Fabulous Death in Him**.

1 Corinthians 15:54-57 "When the perishable has been clothed with the imperishable, and the mortal with immortality, then the saying that is written will come true: Death has been swallowed up in victory. Where, O death, is your victory? Where, O death, is your sting? The sting of death is sin, and the power of sin is the law. But thanks be to God! He gives us the victory through our Lord Jesus Christ."

Now folks, according to our text, the Bible is clear. All of us have a body that will one day what? It's going to die, right? But what happens? When that body dies, we put on what? We put on immortality, right? People, this is why each one of us is going to continue to exist forever in one of two places. Can anybody guess what those two eternal places might be? Hey, that's right! It's heaven or hell, right? But what was the good news? What did it say? The Christian, can not only know that we're going to heaven when we die, but we can actually no longer be afraid of the moment we die! Why? Well, what did it say? We don't need to be afraid of death as a Christian because why? Because thanks be to God Jesus gives us the victory, right?

People, the point is this. Surely the American Church knows this, right? I mean, surely we know there's no stinkin' reason to be afraid of dying. I mean, if Jesus takes care of us when we're on earth, surely He'll take care of us when we depart from this earth, right? People, are you kidding? If you look at most Christians today, it looks like were running just as scared as the rest of this world from the fear of death! Why? Because once again, we have our eyes off of Christ. We've not only forgotten we get a paradise with Him, but we've totally forgotten that even our journey there to be with Him, our death, is actually going to be fabulous. To show you just how fabulous this victory over death really is, let's first look at it's opposite. Let's see how a non-Christian dies without receiving the victory over death in Christ. Here are some of their last words before departing through death's door:

- THOMAS PAYNE: "I would give worlds, if I had them, if the Age of Reason had never been published. O Lord, help me! Christ, help me! Stay with me! It is hell to be left alone!"

- VOLTAIRE: "I am abandoned by God and man! I shall go to hell! O' Jesus Christ!"

- DAVID HUME: The atheist died in utter despair with an awful scene crying out, "I am in the flames!"

- KARL MARX: Was on his deathbed surrounded by candles burning to lucifer and screamed at his nurse who asked him if he had any last words, "Go on, get out! Last words are for fools who haven't said enough."

- NIETZSCHE: Died insane, completely out of his mind.

- SIR THOMAS SCOTT: "Until now I thought there was no God or hell. Now I know there is both, and I am doomed."

- SIR FRANCIS NEWPORT: "Do not tell me there is no God for I know there is one, and that I am in his angry presence! You need not tell me there is no hell, for I already feel my soul slipping into its fires! I know that I am lost forever."[4]

Now folks, I'd say those guys didn't die a very victorious death, how about you? Hey man, forget American Express. It's Jesus you don't want to leave home without, right? Therefore, let's see how the Christian dies who did receive the victory over death through Christ and you tell me if we need to be afraid:

"A year and a half ago, my father-in-law died. He was one of the most godly men I ever met. The day he died, he sat up in bed and spoke. You say, 'So what?' So this.

He was having hardening of the arteries and wasn't talking at all. He sat up in bed at six in the morning. And his wife said he looked at the ceiling and said, 'Oh grave. Oh death. Death where is your sting? Grave where is your victory? Praise be to God who gives me the victory!

Then he waited and he said it again even louder. 'Death where is your sting? Grave where is your victory? Praise be to God who gives me the victory!!

And he paused and for the third time and with full triumph in his voice my mother-in-law said, he yelled laughing at the satanic forces, 'Oh Death where is your sting? Oh grave where is your victory? Praise be to God who gives me the victory!!! And he leaned back in bed and died.

What a way to go! To have lived life fully and intensely. To have seized the opportunity to live out the will of God and to have been alive to the mercies of God. Only then, when the final test comes, can you laugh at satan and tell him that he has no quarters in your life for you belong to the Living Lord!"

Now folks, I personally would like to leave this earth in the same manner as that man did, how about you? People, here's the good news. If you're a Christian, it's true for you too! Why? Because people, God's not only promised to take care of us here on earth, He's promised to take care of us when we leave this earth!

People this is why no matter what goes on in your life there is no stinkin' reason for a Christian to walk around looking like a loser. We don't need to be afraid of sin. We don't need to be afraid of death. We don't even need to be afraid of the actual moment of death. Why? Because we're not a bunch of losers. We belong to Christ. We're His Body. A **Body of Winners**. We've won! Jesus has given us the ultimate victory. Now let's get out there and live like it! Amen?

How to Receive Jesus Christ:

1. Admit your need (I am a sinner).

2. Be willing to turn from your sins (repent).

3. Believe that Jesus Christ died for you on the Cross and rose from the grave.

4. Through prayer, invite Jesus Christ to come in and control your life through the Holy Spirit. (Receive Him as Lord and Savior.)

What to pray:

Dear Lord Jesus,

I know that I am a sinner and need Your forgiveness. I believe that You died for my sins. I want to turn from my sins. I now invite You to come into my heart and life. I want to trust and follow You as Lord and Savior.

In Jesus' name. Amen.

Notes

Chapter One *The Body of Christ*

1. *Story of Phineas Gage,*
   (http://www.deakin.edu.au/hbs/GAGEPAGE/Pgstory.htm)
   (http://www.roadsideamerica.com/attract/VTCAVgage.html)
2. *Origin of An Apple a Day Keeps the Doctor Away*
   (http://www.building19.com/doesan.htm)
3. *Origin of God Bless You*
   (http://www.building19.com/whydowe.htm)
4. *Story of Meatloaf*
   (Source Unknown)
5. *Statistics of American Church False Beliefs*
   (http://www.barna.org)
6. *Origin of Three Blind Mice*
   (http://www.rooneydesign.com/ThreeMice.html)
7. *Origin of Ring Around the Roses*
   (http://www.mother.com/~prdesign/RingRosies.html)
8. *Statistics of American Church False Behavior*
   (http://www.barna.org)
   (http://www.worldmag.com/world/issue/12-06-03/cultural_4.asp)
   (http://www.christianforums.com/t48740&page=5)
9. *Letter Written to Christian Friend*
   (http://www.geocities.com/jmkeeter/blessusa.htm)

Chapter Two *A Body of Brides*

1. *Pastoral Search Committee Criteria*
   (Email Story – Source Unknown)

2. *Seven Phases of a Jewish Marriage Ceremony*
   (www.ldolphin.org/risk/ult.shtml)
3. Roy B. Zuck, *The Speaker's Quote Book,*
   (Grand Rapids: Kregel Publications, 1997, Pg. 206)

Chapter Three   *A Body of One*

1. *Story of Jim and Tammy Faye Bakker*
   (http://en.wikipedia.org/wiki/Jim_Bakker)
   (http://www.rotten.com/library/bio/religion/televangelists/jim-bakker/)
2. *Story of Boy with Cancer*
   (http://biblecenter.com/illustrations/carryingeachothersburdens.htm)
3. *Story of College Boy*
   (Email Story – Source Unknown)

Chapter Four   *A Body of Hope*

1. *Story of Benny Hinn*
   (http://www.aloha.net/~mikesch/tbn.htm)
   (http://www.deceptioninthechurch.com/hinn-07.htm)
   (http://www.csicop.org/si/2002-05/i-files.html)
   (http://www.religionnewsblog.com/6054-.html)
   (http://www.rapidnet.com/~jbeard/bdm/exposes/hinn/general.htm)
   Hank Hanegraaff, *Christianity In Crisis,*
   (Eugene: Harvest House Publishers, 1993, Pg. 11)
2. *Story of John Bunyan*
   (http://www.net153.com/illustrations/index3.html)
3. *Story of Fanny Crosby*
   (http://www.net153.com/illustrations/index3.html)
4. *Story of Woman in Southern California*
   (http://www.net153.com/illustrations/index3.html)
5. *Story of Town that was to be Flooded*
   (http://www.bible.org/illus/h/h-54.htm#TopOfPage)

Chapter Five   *A Body of Joy*

1. *Mixed Up Family*
   (Email Story – Source Unknown)
2. *Quote from Oliver Wendell Holmes*
   (http://www.bible.org/illus/j/j-12.htm#TopOfPage)
3. James S. Hewett, *Illustrations Unlimited*,
   (Wheaton: Tyndale House Publishers, 1988, Pg. 409)
4. *Quote from Billy Sunday*
   (http://www.net153.com/illustrations/christianlifen.shtml)
5. *List of Things to Think About to be Thankful*
   (Email Story – Source Unknown)
6. Roy B. Zuck, *The Speaker's Quote Book*,
   (Grand Rapids: Kregel Publications, 1997, Pg. 216)

Chapter Six   *A Body of Love*

1. *Stella Award Winners*
   (Email Story – Source Unknown)
2. *Things God Won't Ask When We Die*
   (Email Story – Source Unknown)
3. *Story of Rhett Falkner Loving His Enemy (Me)*
   (Actual Account Written by Billy Crone)
4. James S. Hewett, *Illustrations Unlimited*,
   (Wheaton: Tyndale House Publishers, 1988, Pg. 436-437)

Chapter Seven   *A Body of Peace*

1. *Signs of Maturity*
   (Email Story – Source Unknown)
2. *Quote of Going to the Doctor by Faith*
   (http://www.worthydevotions.com)

3. *Story of Thanking God for the Fleas*
   (http://www.worthydevotions.com)
4. *List of Reasons Why People Survived 911*
   (Email Story – Source Unknown)
5. *Story of Abraham Lincoln*
   (http://www.bible.org/illus/g/g-47.htm#TopOfPage)
6. *Story of Ira Sankey*
   (http://www.bible.org/illus/g/g-47.htm#TopOfPage)
7. *Story of B-17 Bomber*
   (http://www.bible.org/illus/g/g-47.htm#TopOfPage)

Chapter Eight   *A Body of Strangers*

1. *Dumb Criminal Behavior*
   (http://www.net153.com/illustrations/index3.html)
   (http://www.dumbcriminalacts.com)
2. *Definition of American Dream*
   (http://www.sermoncentral.com/sermon.asp?SermonID=30963&Contr
   ibutorID=1401)
3. *Story of Communism Versus Materialism*
   (http://www.sermonillustrator.org/illustrator/sermon5/something_far_
   worse.htm)
4. Roy B. Zuck, *The Speaker's Quote Book*,
   (Grand Rapids: Kregel Publications, 1997, Pg. 246)
5. *Quote of Living the Rat Race Life*
   (http://home.pages.at/stargazers/endworld/signs/toandfro.htm)
6. *Story of Being Mentally Handicapped*
   (http://groups.yahoo.com/group/illustrations/message/310)

Chapter Nine   *A Body of Disciples*

1. *Story of Lady Living only for Herself*
   (Email Story – Source unknown)

2. *The So-called Faithful Member*
   (Email Story – Source unknown)
3. Vaughn Shatzer, *History of American Education*,
   (Hagerstown: Word of Prophecy Ministries, 1999, Pgs. 3-9,12-13)
4. *Story of Susanna Wesley*
   (Source Unknown)

Chapter Ten *A Body of Servants*

1. *Mustard Story*
   (Email Story – Source Unknown)
2. James S. Hewett, *Illustrations Unlimited*,
   (Wheaton: Tyndale House Publishers, 1988, Pg. 87)
3. *Story of Son in Need of Mom to Serve Him*
   (Source Unknown)

Chapter Eleven *A Body of Rebels*

1. *Brainless Quotes*
   (Email Story – Source Unknown)
2. James S. Hewett, *Illustrations Unlimited*,
   (Wheaton: Tyndale House Publishers, 1988, Pg. 483)
3. Jeffrey A. Baker, *Cheque Mate the Game of Princes*
   (St. Petersburg: The Baker Group Inc., 1993, Pgs. 206-207)
4. *Statistics Showing Our Lack of Saltiness*
   (http://www.barna.org)
   (http://www.worldmag.com/world/issue/12-06-03/cultural_4.asp)
   (http://www.christianforums.com/t48740&page=5)
5. *Quote from Charles Spurgeon*
   (http://www.crosswalk.com/news/weblogs/mohler/?adate=6/1/2004#1
   265586)
6. *Statistics Showing Our Lack of Brightness*
   (http://www.barna.org)

(http://www.christianitytoday.com/cr/2003/002/7.28.html)
(http://www.christianforums.com/t48740&page=5)
(http://news.bbc.co.uk/go/pr/fr/-/2/hi/entertainment/3229829.stm)
(http://www.crosswalk.com/news/religiontoday/1221952.html)

7. *Quote from Alexis deToqueville*
    (http://www.doctorsenator.com/AlexisdeTocqueville.html)
8. *Story of Son's Blood Saving the World*
    (Email Story – Source Unknown)

Chapter Twelve   *A Body of Worshippers*

1. *Story of Frying Eggs*
    (Email Story – Source Unknown)
2. Roy B. Zuck, *The Speaker's Quote Book*,
    (Grand Rapids: Kregel Publications, 1997, Pgs. 207,208)
3. Roy B. Zuck, *The Speaker's Quote Book*,
    (Grand Rapids: Kregel Publications, 1997, Pg. 383)
4. *Statistics on Entertainment*
    (http://www.cyfc.umn.edu/Documents/H/K/HK1005.html)
    (http://www.cyfc.umn.edu/Documents/C/D/CD1001.html)
    (http://www.cyfc.umn.edu/Documents/C/B/CB1032.html)
    (http://www.midcoast.com/~chestnut/a15.html)
5. *Story of Being Distracted by the devil*
    (Email Story – Source Unknown)
6. *Story of Twenty Dollar Bill and One Dollar Bill*
    (Email Story – Source Unknown)
7. Walter B. Knight, *Knight's Treasury of 2,000 Illustrations*
    (Grand Rapids: Eerdman's Publishing Company, 1963, Pg. 328)

Chapter Thirteen   *A Body of Warriors*

1. *Story God's Never Been Here Before*
    (Email Story – Source Unknown)

2. *What Christians Believe about the Supernatural*
    (http://www.barna.org)
3. Patrick Matrisciana, *devil Worship: The Rise of satanism*,
    (Hemet: Jeremiah Films, 1989, Video)
4. *Story Stopping on the Battlefield*
    (http://www.johnankerberg.org/Articles)
5. *Story Change Your Name*
    (http://www.westminsterpres.com/sermons/sermon_06-22-03.htm)

Chapter Fourteen   *A Body of Witnesses*

1. *Weird Things in Life*
    (Email Story – Source Unknown)
2. *What Should We Pray For?*
    (Created by Billy Crone)
3. *Story of Church Buildings Next to Cemeteries*
    (http://www.worthynews.com)
4. *Can You Imagine?*
    (Created by Billy Crone)
5. *What is Hell Like?*
    (Study Derived from Online Bible Study Tools)
    (http://bible.crosswalk.com)
6. Joe Schimmel, *They Sold Their Souls for Rock-n-Roll*,
    (Simi Valley: Fight the Good Fight Ministries, 2001, Video)

Chapter Fifteen   *A Body of Winners*

1. *Story of Jim Jones*
    (http://www.religioustolerance.org/dc_jones.htm)
    (http://www.cnn.com/US/9811/18/jonestown.anniv.01/)
2. *No More HMO's*
    (Email Story – Source Unknown)
3. *What is Heaven Like?*

(Study Derived from Online Bible Study Tools)
(http://bible.crosswalk.com)
4. Dr. Kent Hovind, *The Garden of Eden*, Video
   (Pensacola: Creation Science Evangelism, 1996)
5. *Last Words of Non-Christians*
   (http://www.anzwers.org/free/lastwords/)